# Creative Industries and Digital Transformation in China

Sabine Chrétien-Ichikawa · Karolina Pawlik
Editors

# Creative Industries and Digital Transformation in China

palgrave
macmillan

*Editors*
Sabine Chrétien-Ichikawa
ESSCA School of Management
Shanghai, China

Karolina Pawlik
USC-SJTU Institute of Cultural and Creative Industry
Shanghai, China

ISBN 978-981-19-3048-5    ISBN 978-981-19-3049-2 (eBook)
https://doi.org/10.1007/978-981-19-3049-2



This Palgrave Macmillan imprint is published by the registered company Springer Nature Singapore Pte Ltd.
The registered company address is: 152 Beach Road, #21-01/04 Gateway East, Singapore 189721, Singapore

# Contents

# Notes on Contributors

**Thomas Amadieu** is a French associate professor at the Shanghai campus of the *ESSCA School of Management*, within the Economics, Law and Society Department. He holds a Ph.D. in Sociology from Sorbonne University (CNU 19) in the field of gambling, risk-taking, and addiction. He is also a research associate at GEMASS (CNRS/Sorbonne University) and at the EU*Asia Institute. He is involved in research projects adopting a comparative perspective between China and France, in the field of youth work attitudes, representations of sustainability and market dynamics in gaming (gambling, video games, eSport). His work has been published in various scientific outlets (*Revue Française de Sociologie*, *Agora Débats/Jeunesse*, *Droits. Revue française de théorie, de philosophie et de culture juridique*, *Sciences du jeu*, PUPS, Presses universitaires du Septentrion, Armand Colin, Cambridge Scholars Publishing). He is the author, with Nicolas Framont, of the book *Les citoyens ont de bonnes raisons de ne pas voter* (Citizens have good reasons not to vote).

**Sabine Chrétien-Ichikawa** is a French researcher based in Shanghai since 2012, doing field research in China since 2005. She started her career in the fashion industry in Italy, as a designer, and moved into managerial positions in small and large companies, in New York, Tokyo, and Paris (such as Kenzo (LVMH Group), ELLE Japan, Cacharel). After embracing an academic career, she focused on the birth of Shanghai city as a potential fashion capital and a creative hub, under the influence of Japan since the nineteenth century. Later, she broadened her scope to the creative economy in emerging markets, as she witnessed the need for a local cultural and creative environment to blossom before original fashion brands could gain world fame. Her current research investigates the rise of sustainable consumption in China, leadership for sustainable fashion, and purpose-driven management in the creative industries. She holds a Ph.D. in Business History from EHESS (Ecole des Hautes Etudes en Sciences Sociales), an M.B.A. in International Luxury Brand Management from ESSEC Business School, and a BA in Fashion Design from ESMOD, all in Paris. She runs the M.Sc. in EU-Asia Luxury Marketing in *Essca School of Management*, between Shanghai and Paris since 2016, mentoring consulting projects for French and Chinese luxury companies.

**Gabriele Goretti** is an architect, designer, and researcher in product and fashion design strategy and luxury goods market. His work focuses on the relationships between design strategies and advanced manufacturing processes, including design-driven innovation based on technology innovation and traceability. He earned his Ph.D. at "L.Vanvitelli" University (Naples, Italy) in Industrial Design, Environment and History. Currently, he is Associate Professor at Jiangnan University in Wuxi (China), where he is leading the Brand Future UX Design Lab and teaches Design Management and Design Methodologies and Principles courses. Moreover, he is an invited professor at ESSCA Business School/Shanghai, where he teaches Design Innovation for Luxury Markets. Previously, he has also worked at the University of Florence, the Istituto Europeo di Design in Florence, the Nanjing University School of Art, and the Design Lab at Maker Place of Nanjing University.

**Alexandre Ouairy** is a doctoral researcher in the Department of History of Art and Archaeology at SOAS University of London. He investigates Chinese contemporary art history, under the supervision of Professor Shane McCausland. His research explores the transformation of contemporary art practices in China by examining the interplay between artists, institutions, the market economy, and censorship. His interests lie in cultural and visual studies, critical theory, aesthetics, and practices of the self in contemporary China. Prior to SOAS, he had extensive experience in China as an art history lecturer at the Shanghai Theatre Academy, an artist, and a creative director. He possesses a National Diploma of Art (DNAP) and a National Higher Diploma of Plastic Expression (DNSEP) from École Nationale Supérieure d'Art de Grenoble, France. He has exhibited in institutions such as Lyon Biennial, Palais de Tokyo, and Shanghai Biennial Off.

**Karolina Pawlik** comes from Poland. She holds a Ph.D. in Cultural Studies from the University of Silesia. She is an anthropologist, a scholar of Chinese visual culture, and a poet. Based in Shanghai since 2012, she has taught and supervised students in a number of international university programs related to design, creative economy, and cultural heritage. Her main research interests include calligraphy, graphic design, Chinese modernization, and urban lighting.

# List of Figures

CHAPTER 1

# Introduction

*Karolina Pawlik*

## 1 Introductory Thoughts

Writing about contemporary China is never easy, given the pace of its transformation as well as the amount of cultural and political variables at play, all of which require careful consideration. The COVID-19 pandemic presented yet more challenges; on the one hand, it accelerated many changes, while on the other hand it undercut what, in certain cases, seemed to be established trajectories for China's cultural development and international cooperation. So much has been interrupted or suspended, and so much may yet become alternated in flows into the near future. And yet, in many ways, it is exactly these challenging conditions that make this collection of scholarly essays particularly relevant, as an account of a rapidly shifting cultural reality. Even though it is impossible to determine the future of Chinese creative industries, there is much to inquire about their current condition and the trajectory of their development.

K. Pawlik (✉)
USC-SJTU Institute of Cultural and Creative Industry, Shanghai, China
e-mail: karolinapawlik88@gmail.com



S. Chrétien-Ichikawa and K. Pawlik (eds.), *Creative Industries and Digital Transformation in China*,
https://doi.org/10.1007/978-981-19-3049-2_1

This book consists of contributions made by five China-based European researchers, each with interdisciplinary backgrounds and a focus on the social sciences. With affiliations with various higher education institutions in China over extended periods of time, we have had valuable opportunities to bridge the perceptions of insiders and outsiders. Through teaching, research, consultancy, and our own creative practices, we have been able to actively contribute our expertise to the growing sector of Chinese creative industries. This book is a tangible outcome of our extensive exercise in mediating and translating between cultures, as well as reimagining the global cultural and creative industries scene. Combining the advantages of field research and frequent movement between Europe and China, as well as our personal transcultural experiences and encounters in daily life, we offer nuanced insights into the ever-transforming cultural realm of contemporary China.

Each chapter discusses a different cultural practice or phenomenon of major importance within China's creative industries, and pursues intellectual inquiry as shaped by a different sensitivity. Given the relative specificity of contemporary Chinese creative industries, we felt it suitable to include a variety of voices, interests, and concerns. We hope, in this way, to mirror in book's composition and style, the fluid, kaleidoscopic nature of creative industries that are rapidly evolving under China's changing conditions.

Different as they may be, the chapters in this book all focus on cultural practices rather than cultural policies, as the authors reflect on the potential of ongoing technological transformations to reimagine and reshape Chinese society and cultural heritage. Through the lenses of art, design, fashion, gaming, and media industries, our research highlights processes of innovation and reinvention in the making, and the impact such processes have on Chinese cultural values, including on urban and national narratives. We are interested in China, first of all, as culture and society, not market. The growth of companies and industries, changes in creation and consumption patterns, and the reshaping of dominant discourse and imagery are thus placed within a broader historical and socio-cultural context.

Through our research endeavor, we join the efforts of scholars who have paid increasing attention to the development of creative industries in China, as well as those who are particularly interested in the impact of digital transformations (Keane, 2009, 2013; Moeran, 2021; Montgomery, 2011; O'Connor & Gu 2020). In relation to various cultural practices, we explore the emergence of new trends that have been enabled by the power of digital technology. We seek particularly to understand the commodification of culture, as fueled by contemporary consumption and social media-oriented technology, which enhances both purchase power and a desire for constant entertainment.

## 2 Creative Industries in China

Since the late 1970s, the world has been watching China's rapid transition from planned economy to market economy, from an export-led growth model toward greater reliance on domestic consumption, and from reliance on heavy industry and low-cost manufacturing toward an economy in which the production of goods and services with high levels of aesthetic and semiotic content is perceived as both a major economic sector and a source for competitive advantage globally. Often the content being produced today is more valued for its intangible qualities than its tangible ones.

Chinese cultural and creative industries have already become one of the pillars of the national economy. Cultural resources have been turned into economic capital by many countries, and yet China stands out as a state with explicit connectivity between expanded cultural influence and political gains for the country. The close connection between culture, creative industries, and the expansion of soft power has become clearer each year since Xi Jinping 习近平 came to power in 2012. However, this course has in fact been set since the 16th CCP Congress in 2002, when China's cultural system reform (CSR) was launched (Keane & Zhao, 2014). With culture linked directly to national power and international competitiveness, cultural and creative industries have now been elevated to the level of national strategy and approached as an important means to promote the development of socialist culture with Chinese characteristics. As a result, three particularly significant aspects of China's anticipated development (creativity, technological autonomy, and the consolidation of national identity) are crucial for the expansion of China's cultural and creative industries in accordance with a specifically Chinese destiny.

Assigning strong political and patriotic dimensions to cultural and creative industries in China requires navigating multiple constraints to comply with official guidelines and satisfy target audiences. As Michael Keane (2013) has observed, since 2007 creativity in China has been perceived as a resource to serve the nation, and can be tied to patriotic attitude (p. 79). Since products and trends have to be endorsed within a broader framework of national virtues and strengths, the creators and the state are constantly challenged to harmonize the country's core socialist values with materialism that benefits the national economy, while maintaining audience satisfaction. Viewed from a distance, this environment often appears to be simply a powerful state restricting artists and innovators who struggle against multiple constraints. Yet seen from within, a much more complex set of power relations and creative forces is revealed, as well as multiple fascinating frictions within and across power lines. The digital lives of Chinese people remain dynamic and rich, despite state control and political constraints, and this nuance demands scholarly attention.

Over the years, creative industries in China have become an arena for the convergence and competition of domestic and foreign forces. As China's position has grown globally, it has also begun to actively reshape international order and the global market. Increasingly, China aspires to compete in various sectors, including international creative industries, through a distinctive, Chinese creative vision and model of development. In this way, China intends to use creative industries to brand Chinese culture for the world and, ultimately, enhance their soft power. This has produced prolific friction, as on the one hand China has to negotiate cooperation and connection within the global creative economy; on the other hand, it works to maintain an autonomous system rooted in specific cultural and political values, in order to serve its own goals. Many of the opposing forces at play that define the evolution of China's creative industries may sound like clichés dating back to the Republican Era (1912–1949) and China's first attempts to define its own vision of modernity. However, they remain valid and under constant negotiation as China enters the third decade of the twenty-first century as well. Among them, and particularly worth mentioning, are nationalism and cosmopolitanism, socialism and consumerism, China and the West, China and the world, tradition and the future, heritage and technology. In other words, both the Chinese state and the agents contributing to the development of creative industries in China strive to obtain the ultimate balance between cultural conservatism and cutting-edge innovation, all while cultivating "Chinese cultural characteristics" within broad transnational networks. We inquire in this book about what new cultural meanings are being crafted at these crossroads.

## 3 Digital Transformation

China takes pride in its ancient roots, but at the same time culture is actively reshaped by China's ambition to transform itself and the world through unprecedented digital infrastructure. What seems particularly impactful for the development of creative industries is the fact that, since 2010, China has been speedily transforming into a smartphone-driven society. Making great leaps beyond an environment of personal computer technology, the popularity of increasingly locally produced smartphones sees even the most underprivileged members of the society owning handheld smart devices. Such progress has evaded desktop and laptop computers and, instead, embraced and been fueled by ubiquitous mobile apps. Thus, in at least every major Chinese city, it has become the norm for people to carry nothing else, supported entirely by their smartphone. Indeed, it is not uncommon to notice people eating with chopsticks in one hand at a restaurant while swiping through their phones with the other. Or on the way to work, a commuter may be saying the rosary with one hand while holding their smartphone with the other, all the while remaining quite absorbed by a short-video app. Elderly Chinese urbanites remember a time when there was one phone available for multiple households; they are now facing a reality in which it is extremely difficult—if not impossible—to navigate through the city (and especially between cities) without a decent smartphone. Smartphones do not merely facilitate communication or provide access to information—they transform lifestyles and creative processes, as well as affect consumption and production modes. They reshape the values, relationships, and routines of daily life.

China has paid a high price for its absence in the world's first three industrial revolutions and, as a result, has become fully committed to maintaining a position at the forefront of the Fourth Industrial Revolution, which blurs the boundaries between the physical, digital, and biological worlds. Fear of being left behind again can be seen on every level, from governmental policies ensuring steady technological progress to China's public enthusiasm for new technologies and an often uncritical engagement with smart devices. With incredible pace and faith, China heads into total reliance on technology in all aspects of life and governance, on a level unprecedented in human history. Such ambition takes many forms and is manifested in different ways and scales, from developing super-apps and enforcing cashless payments, to encounters with robot butlers in hotel lobbies or restaurants, to launching a virtual mall via a WeChat Mini Program. Immersive urban light shows celebrate yet another phase of accomplished modernity, with all sorts of technology from holograms to drone displays and synchronized dynamic illuminations lighting up the skylines of smart cities. Such enormous trust in a digital future inevitably shapes and transforms many existing and emerging sectors of creative industries, from cultural values and imagination, to art and design practice, to social interactions, branding, and sales strategies.

China's strong investment in the development of technological infrastructure and innovation is underpinned by an ambition known as "technological leapfrogging," in other words, by "omitting the industrial phase with the help of information and communication technologies to catch up with Western developed societies in the Information Age" (Liu, 2011, p. 42). If growing information technology is perceived as an important national goal and a source of pride, it is at least, to some extent, because of the promise it brings: that China may finally heal from the disgrace experienced for a hundred years following the Opium Wars, the "Century of Humiliation" (1839–1949), when it was unable to compete with technologically advanced colonial powers. Indeed, as Fengshu Liu (2011), author of *Urban Youth in China: Modernity, the Internet and the Self*, noted, the Chinese discourse about modernization "revolves around a wish to 'restore' power to the Middle Kingdom by re-achieving its technological supremacy" (p. 42).

While this modernization and digital transformation brings genuine benefits to many citizens, there are glaring concerns. New technologies and especially the assembly of apps promising increased convenience in daily life—covering potential needs from quick food delivery to emotional support—accelerate the privatization of life, a condition already progressing in the schemes of industrialization and urbanization. To some extent, these elements have become mutually enhancing: technology facilitates alienation by enabling unprecedented workloads for people in various professions, which in turn leads to an even greater integration of technology into daily life in order to manage simple life tasks and make an attempt to release increasing emotional burdens. Other major concerns involve the capacity of legal regulations to keep pace with innovation and the rapid transformation of people's lives by AI. Privacy and lack of full transparency with regard to gathering and processing personal data are real concerns, even if public safety or pandemic control, for example, seems to validate certain surveillance solutions. Issues in rising inequality and even exploitation also appear irrevocably linked to rapid and uneven technological advancement, for example where ultimate efficiency meets human limitations. Accidents like floods that result in disruptions of electricity supply and networks only highlight the issues with a total reliance on smart devices, which may actually increase vulnerability and give rise to disasters. With modernization, there are certainly always substantial ethical and pragmatic issues to consider.

Various other concerns become clear upon examination of the actions undertaken by the Chinese government to secure a desirable digital future. These have to do with maintaining socialist values (such as collectivism, altruism, and patriotism), securing national cohesion, monitoring the *wanghong* 网红 economy (China's digital economy, based on influencer marketing in social media), crafting desirable social identities in compliance with the country's needs and long-term plans, and limiting the exposure of citizens to the ideologies and cultural influences considered harmful by the state. Cautious management of technological transformation is, from this perspective, about managing the nation's future, which must be built by productive, reliable, and morally unblemished Chinese subjects (Liu, 2011, pp. 103–107).

What seems to revolve around prudence, precaution, and conservatism also implies an attempt to take full advantage of the unprecedented opportunities technology offers in pursuit of major national goals. More specifically, technology clearly has the power to unite people for a common goal or around certain beliefs, and therefore may be manipulated to consolidate national identity. Furthermore, technology may be used in an effort to nurture cultural awareness domestically, while improving China's image abroad. In this sense, for quite some time already, creative industries in China appear entrusted with a strategic responsibility: to help China develop a new cultural and national identity into the new century.

## 4 Chapters' Overview

This book consists of seven chapters exploring interrelations between technology, creativity, and culture in Shanghai or similar major urban settings, in relation to the most privileged and affluent part of the Chinese society. Each author contributes in a different way to the overall picture of the scale and profoundness of the rapid transformation of Chinese urban and social fabric, and the impact it has or likely will have in the near future on the country's industries, identities, and dominant narratives.

Chapter 2, *Keep the Living Practice Alive: Calligraphy, Commodification, and Postliterate Culture*, figures calligraphy, a cultural practice of particular significance in China, that is taking place within the changing urban environment and creative economy context of China today. I discuss the entanglement of handwriting and technology to outline important objectives for maintaining a balance between efforts to brand calligraphy within creative industries, preserve it as a significant part of Chinese heritage, and carry it into the future as a vital creative and spiritual practice.

Chapter 3, *From Rehabilitated Factories to Cyberspace: The Migration of the Art Ecosystem in Shanghai*, examines the last 30 years of artistic production and exhibitions in Shanghai from the 1990s to the 2020s in the face of a changing institutional landscape. Alexandre Ouairy discusses the emergence of contemporary art practices and their evolution into increasingly virtual formats, largely forced by the dynamics of urban redevelopment in China. He raises a number of significant issues related to the commercialization of art, China's global creative ambitions, and complex relationships between the state, the artists, and consumers.

Chapter 4, *Addictive Technologies? The Moral and Normative Dynamics Shaping the Chinese Gaming Culture*, looks into the rise of the gaming industry in China and uses this sector of major importance for China to inquire about some of the moral and normative aspects strongly embedded in creative economy in China. In Thomas Amadieu's analysis, the gaming industry becomes a fascinating case study to reflect on distinct Chinese patterns in channeling or enhancing creation and consumption, and the implications it has for business, government, and users. This is particularly interesting given China's global ambitions for this sector of great economic and ideological importance.

Chapter 5, *Mediatization in Fashion: A Focus on the Rise of Reflective Emotions Within China's Digital Ecosystem*, offers an overview on the digital landscape in China relating to the role of media in the fashion system. Gabrielle Goretti focuses his attention on the crucial role of emotions in fashion mediatization in China. He discusses various foreign and Chinese patterns and scenarios in order to understand the impact of China's technological advancement on the transformation of information and communication, and the ongoing commodification of feelings.

Chapter 6, ***Shanghai Fashion and Post-1990s Youth Through the Phygital Lens***, examines Shanghai fashion through three dimensions: the physical, digital, and social dimensions. Sabine Chrétien-Ichikawa outlines opportunities and challenges for the fashion industry in the rapidly changing urban environment. She combines fragments from the past and future, and her analysis offers a rich array of notions and factors shaping the scene, including the tastes and sensitivities of young urban consumers within physical spaces and online.

We do not aspire to provide a general picture of China's growth, a definite record of China's history, or propositions for a long-term future. Having experienced the complexity of this country firsthand, including the pace of change and variety of factors which may impact the direction of further growth and expansion, we choose instead to focus on particular phenomena and practices, to add to the record of what is actually occurring in Chinese society now. This volume is presented to the reader without the ambition to provide decisive answers, but rather with the hope that it may open a meaningful conversation. This conversation will be continued with a broader audience within creative industries and educational institutions, and thereby facilitate deep and genuinely transcultural understanding between China and the world.

## References


Keane, M. (2009). *Created in China: The great new leap forward.* Routledge.

Keane, M. (2013). *Creative industries in China: Art, design and media.* Polity.

Keane, M., & Zhao, E. J. (2014). The reform of the cultural system: Culture, creativity and innovation in China. In H. K. Lee & L. Lim (Eds.), *Cultural Policies in East Asia.* Palgrave Macmillan.

Liu, F. (2011). *Urban youth in China: Modernity, the internet and the self.* Routledge.

Moeran, B. (2021). *Creative and cultural industries in East Asia: An introduction.* Routledge.

Montgomery, L. (2011). *China's creative industries: Copyright, social network markets and the business of culture in a digital age.* Edward Elgar Publishing.

O'Connor, J., & Gu, X. (2020). *Red creative: Culture and modernity in China.* Intellect Ltd.

CHAPTER 2

# Keep the Living Practice Alive: Calligraphy, Commodification, and Postliterate Culture

*Karolina Pawlik*

## 1 Shifting Meanings and Contexts

What does it mean for brush practice to remain alive in twenty-first-century China, following the various challenges and disruptions it has overcome since late-nineteenth century? (Barrass, 2002). This question returns to me often in different ways: during university conferences, exhibitions, art events, and even on daily walks in my old neighborhood in Shanghai's Hongkou district. For instance, I think about brush practice when I see children meticulously copying characters in the small private calligraphy school, as they are performing their extracurricular activity. After these classes, the children are photographed with the characters they have written, and these photos circulate on social media. Once, their young teacher engaged me in a friendly conversation and told me, "Now that the Chinese economy has developed, Chinese people can focus

K. Pawlik (✉)
USC-SJTU Institute of Cultural and Creative Industry, Shanghai, China
e-mail: karolinapawlik88@gmail.com



S. Chrétien-Ichikawa and K. Pawlik (eds.), *Creative Industries and Digital Transformation in China*,
https://doi.org/10.1007/978-981-19-3049-2_2

on culture. My father was so poor he didn't have enough food – how could he think of Chinese culture?" (Interview, Shanghai, March 2020). The teacher had quit his former career in business to develop platforms to teach calligraphy. He ended up inviting me to become his student and offered me the prospect of great success as "a Douyin[1] celebrity with many fans appreciating a foreign woman skilled in writing with the brush." I refused because I already have a teacher who helps me to pursue my calligraphy path in less ostentatious ways.

In another instance, several evenings in a row I saw a man practicing calligraphy inside a small shop selling summer sleeping mats and pillows. I reflected again on what it means to pass down this brush and ink tradition. He sat at a tiny table, and when I began to talk to him, he immediately made the assumption that his calligraphy would pale in comparison with mine, given that I am a university instructor, and he is merely a vendor. He positioned himself within traditional social hierarchies and thought his activity was unexceptional. In my view, however, there are significant differences between practicing calligraphy in a quiet spacious studio, either as a lifelong intellectual pursuit, or for the sake of personal fame and financial gains, and his humble, honest endeavor, pursued in between receiving customers in his seasonal shop. In many ways, he may be closer to the core of this practice, than many renowned calligraphers in China's contemporary art world, because his practice centers on the cultivation of self-discipline and spiritual growth. Sometimes, his carefully handwritten ink inscriptions offer the names and prices of the different goods on sale in his shop, as they used to everywhere in the Shanghai streets of the past. Each time I pass, his signage inspires me to reflect on major differences between such characters handwritten in ink for commercial purposes and those commonly displayed on banners or signboards advertising dining or shopping venues across the city, which often fit into the brush aesthetics, but lack any connection with the human hand.

The generation who used the brush in school on a daily basis is still alive, although they have been forced to switch—at least partly—from the brush to digital writing within a few decades. The word "tablet" nowadays is quite unlikely to bring to people's minds elaborately carved, at times weathered stone calligraphy tablets. More pertinent may be the fact

[1] Douyin is a social media app for creating and sharing short music videos and live-broadcasting, founded in 2016. It is similar to TikTok and was created by the same Beijing-based internet company, Bytedance.

that a troublesome question for contemporary urbanites is not "When was the last time you wrote with a brush?" but "When did you last write with a pen, with your hand, on paper?" One of my most memorable text messages on WeChat, in which digital characters were supplemented as usual with a few emojis, was from a Chinese colleague of mine. This individual, a graphic designer and researcher of typography, confessed, "It's been a long time since I wrote characters. I don't know if they forgot me or I forgot them." It can be interpreted as confession of 'character amnesia' (提笔忘字), but it can be also taken more broadly as sign of awareness that, due to the common use of keyboards and screens, many people maintain very complicated relationships with characters. It is important to emphasize this complexity, because the decline of handwriting in the digital era does not simply mean that Chinese people's relationship with characters is dead. Linguistic invention pursued with digital tools and for online communication takes fascinating new forms, powered by the current political, aesthetic, and transcultural setting. The script is alive, but it takes increasingly digital forms or forms heavily mediated by technology, and largely influenced by animation, cartoons, graffiti, and digital art. It certainly creates unforeseen opportunities for the visual evolution of the script, but also places calligraphy in a very challenging visual and creative context.

In 2009, Chinese calligraphy was inscribed on the UNESCO Representative List of the Intangible Cultural Heritage of Humanity. The Representative List, which presented 76 intangible cultural heritage elements that year, stated that:

> Chinese calligraphy has always been more than simply a tool for communication, incorporating as it does the element of artistry for which the practice is still valued in an age of ballpoint pens and computers. Indeed, calligraphy is no longer the basic tool of intellectuals and officials but has become the preserve of professional artisans and amateur enthusiasts. (UNESCO, 2009)

The document recognized not only the importance of calligraphy in its distinctive Chinese form as an important channel for the appreciation of traditional culture, but also as a source of pride and pleasure for the Chinese people, and an embodiment of key aspects of the country's intellectual and artistic heritage (UNESCO, 2009). Indeed, the Chinese state has invested great effort in recent years, both at home and abroad, to popularize calligraphy practice in the form of classes and exhibitions; Chinese people also take much pride in these efforts. Moreover, as part of the broader search for a distinct Chinese visual identity, the amount of innovative design invoking ink aesthetics has been steadily increasing across branding and advertising in recent years. The fundamental question to raise, then, is whether such efforts actively contribute to passing down the active skill and spirit of calligraphy, or merely nurture a certain aura of attachment to memories of a glorious cultural past and great dead masters.

In this study, I offer a critical enquiry into the opportunities for brush practice to fit into writing routines in contemporary China, where, as Micheal Keane (2021) has aptly noticed, "Many people use their thumbs more than hands, they use emojis instead of expressing real thoughts in words." One major challenge faced by brush practice is the evolution of communication and writing modes, triggered by intrusion of new technology. Another one has to do with the rapid development of creative industries and cultural heritage becoming a bigger driver in the Chinese market. Within the creative economy framework, calligraphy is often approached not as much as a spiritual practice or intellectual pursuit, but instead as a prestigious and appealing component of Chinese heritage which, through more or less superficial references, can add value in different sectors of cultural and creative industries. It is worrisome to observe how creative content and cultural storytelling are increasingly developed to facilitate commodification of Chinese traditions, in accordance with common requests for constant attraction, visually thrilling consumption and online entertainment, suitable for social media and ideally appealing to mass audience both in China and abroad.

## 2 Calligraphy and Technology

The swift development of science and technology, as well as rapid economic growth in China, has had a profound impact on living traditions such as brush practice. Many cultural practices, which are now required to fit into new conceptual frameworks, have become closely integrated with technology and expanding creative industries. Michael Keane, who pioneered the study of creative industries in China, observed as early as 2013 that the Chinese government supported the convergence of technology and culture, expecting Chinese culture to benefit from new media, partly by turning traditional culture into commercializable forms (Keane,

2013, p. 46). This objective has only become more clear with each passing year, with many legacies of profound cultural connotation reinvented through projects blending art and science, heritage, and virtual reality (VR). Given this trend, a critical inquiry into how ongoing digital transformations reshape major cultural practices is necessary to ensure these cultural practices are not diluted and lost in the future.

In my understanding, in order to protect China's living traditions as active cultural practices, as well as secure a solid foundation for the cultural and creative industries in twenty-first-century China, a strong, clear, and genuine connection between innovative technology and China's cultural legacy is crucial. For instance, it is necessary to honestly address the merger between traditional culture and technologies. Is traditional culture expected to harmonize with rapidly emerging new technologies, or should technology respect cultural values and comply with the spirit of said culture? In China's aspiration for global leadership, in both technology and culture, which of the two is perceived as the revered core? Although the public may be increasingly surrounded and conditioned by technology, I would argue that, first of all, they remain embedded in culture, which predates the current technology. Therefore, this legacy should not be perceived merely through the lens of potential compliance with new technology. In fact, calligraphy has the potential to evolve in multiple ways, subjected to technology or coexisting with it, and may become in the future something other, and even something more, than it is now.

A greater threat posed to brush practice is that, as more people become familiar with its form as mediated by technology, they are unaware of how one ultimately transforms the other. With little reflection on how or why this blending is happening within a particular creative or commercial endeavor, or what the repercussions are on various levels, brush practice as a living cultural legacy seems to be taken for granted. The turn away from patient handwriting towards more efficient or thrilling, screen-mediated experiences often tends to be accepted as an organic progression of tradition, usually in accordance with the noble intentions behind such endeavors. However, without sufficient cautious reflection, such efforts may depart from tradition entirely. Relinquishing the actual core of brush practice, and reshaping—not to say distorting—the understanding of this cultural heritage, for the sake of short-term gains in terms of financial benefits or soft power, in fact implies discontinuity. In order to protect the intangible aspect of calligraphy practice, it is urgent to make a critical distinction between the invisible core of a cultural practice (intangible heritage) and digital constructs (immaterial creative projects). Placing focus entirely on the visible traces of the brush, which then become digitized, may easily result in losing the primary depth and opulence of this bodily practice in the following generations.

Calligraphy in China was never merely about artwork, or social recognition of talented calligraphers, or art heritage; therefore, appreciation or promotion of calligraphy 's heritage cannot be sufficient on its own. It is necessary to interrogate comprehensive solutions to maintain the inheritance of the central aspect of calligraphy: the handwriting practice itself. There has been a growing awareness of the importance of improving handwriting skills at the primary education level, mainly by alternating the curriculum and arranging various competitions and exams to motivate children to practice calligraphy. The major challenge ahead is to maintain this handwriting habit for adults, who are often busy with work or attracted to less traditional and less challenging forms of leisure.

In this chapter, I conduct a closer analysis of Chinese calligraphy practice in the context of new technologies currently encompassing Chinese cities. My curiosity is driven by the desire to understand what happens when a culture with a venerated handwriting practice at its core strives to reinvent itself as a digital culture, boldly embracing new technologies to shape the ways in which people interact, behave, think, and communicate. In order to advocate for calligraphy as a worthwhile, or even thriving, practice in twenty-first-century China, one must understand the broader context, in which even ordinary handwriting with a pen or pencil is diminishing, and printed analog materials are challenged by their digital equivalents and online services. This essay is a preliminary study on this topic, and part of a much broader ongoing research endeavor aimed at clarifying the impact of new technologies on the perception and evolution of such significant components of Chinese heritage as calligraphy, ink painting, and classical gardens.

Cyberculture impacts the social perception and transformation of brush practice in multiple ways, including digital reinterpretations of old ink scrolls in virtual reality, various social media filters, or editing applications to 'beautify' videos depicting calligraphers and their writing practice. The use of graphics software like Adobe Illustrator allows designers to achieve brush-like effects without having to scan any actual brushwork. I will focus my attention on the primary question of what happens to the writing hand in this new and constantly evolving urban, social, and technological environment. Central to my attention is a human being holding a brush in a skilled hand. I choose to use the term "brush practice," because it emphasizes the action while avoiding the necessity of immediately judging whether a certain practitioner deserves to be considered a calligrapher according to the traditional standards. Moreover, "calligraphy" is a term that, in a contemporary context, involves great experimentation, and at times pushes the boundaries so far as to entirely discard the brush.

Research on calligraphy tends to be situated most often within art history or aesthetics. However, in my own research on brush practice, following scholars like Yuehping Yen, I apply anthropological perspective and approach writing as a social and cultural practice in contemporary China (Yen, 2005). As an anthropologist of writing, I study the cultural history of China through the lens of the transformation of its writing—from oracle bone inscriptions to the new, currently unfolding chapter of writing intertwined with advanced technologies and AI. I am, therefore, not interested in complete artworks as much as the handwriting practice itself.

## 3 Towards Cyberculture and Postliterate Culture

For centuries, Chinese writing (including the script, the writing practice with the brush and Chinese written heritage) has remained the main tool of differentiation between Chinese people and foreigners. Chinese characters and writing culture have unified China across time and space (Yen, 2005, p. 16), and even during periods of foreign conquest, Chinese language/script and its link to spiritual Chinese culture never vanished. Chinese characters have never been entirely replaced by another language, not even in the colonized ports after the Opium Wars (1839–1860) (Lee, 1999, p. 310). The significance of this script for Chinese people today is indeed such that accomplished Chinese designer and ink practitioner Pan Jianfeng 潘剑锋 did not exaggerate when he once remarked, "Chinese culture will never be destroyed as long as the language and the writing remain" (Online interview, October 2021).

From its earliest iteration, writing in China has not just been a form of communication, but also a means to connect with the spiritual world. As Gordon S. Barrass (2002) noted, in the early stages of use and development of the Chinese script during the Shang Dynasty (1600 BC–1046

BC), "written characters had been a gift from Heaven to humans, but one that could be understood only by those who were divinely inspired, that is, the shamans and the rulers who employed them" (p. 16). The unification of the Chinese Empire (221 BC), and the increasing separation of politics from religion and rituals, as well as the solidification of mechanisms of state bureaucracy, resulted in the widespread use of writing for secular and administrative reasons (Gernet, 2008, p. 376). Literacy spread further through society with the systematization of text-based civil service examinations as the primary means of official recruitment since the Sui Dynasty (581–618), which turned mastery of the classical language, classical canon, and calligraphy into a gateway to political authority, social status, and economic security. For centuries since, the privileged relationship to culture and writing has been tied to privileged positions in society. It was not until the start of the twentieth century that the popularization of literacy was significantly developed in China.

In Chinese tradition, handwriting was an art form in itself. Text was appreciated and valued not necessarily for what was written, but how it was written. Elegantly handwritten text brought both visual and intellectual pleasure, and was it also perceived as "a mirror of the moral quality of the person who wrote it" (Barrass, 2002, p. 20). For centuries, in order to prove high moral rectitude and a well-formed personality, any candidate aspiring to the intellectual and political elite of China had to demonstrate high calligraphy skills. Commenting on the thorough and time-consuming handwriting exercises performed in local Chinese schools, which have not changed much since their inception, Cecilia Lindqvist (2008) remarked that handwriting practice may be considered a kind of ethical and cultural training. Indeed, in parallel to acquiring correct and beautiful writing skills, these exercises impose a lasting practice of patience and endurance. Furthermore, they also indirectly teach children about prevailing societal values of interdependence, adaptation, harmony, and communal relations between part and whole (Lindqvist, 2008, p. 397). Contemporary Chinese artist Xu Bing 徐冰, who has devoted his art to language and writing issues, made similar comments in an interview, recalling how his father made him do a page of calligraphy a day. "At that time," Xu says, "I thought he just wanted me to have beautiful calligraphy, but now I know that kind of training and method was a kind of cultural control – it inspires young people with culture, about being square, very tight, following the rules" (Ch'ien, 2008, p. 65). When he spoke to me of the harmonious movements underpinning Chinese society far beyond the calligraphy table, Pan Jianfeng emphasized the importance of learning the movement of writing. Movements that have the ability to unite gathered people with one other and with their surroundings, and which can take a form of tracing the brush along the page, as well as passing food with chopsticks during a family dinner, or placing mahjong tiles on the table. Pan concluded, "Who doesn't understand the movement of the brush, cannot understand China" (Interview, Shanghai, April 2013).

Calligraphy has acquired profound meaning since ancient times, which has been sustained throughout all the upheaval and modernization campaigns of the twentieth century. Special attention must be paid to the current rapid growth of cyberculture and gradual, yet most likely inevitable, transition towards postliterate culture in China. Calligraphy, which for centuries remained at the center of Chinese culture as a significant creative practice and a channel to pass on spiritual values and knowledge, now finds itself at the edge. As postliterate culture rises, it increasingly determines the shape of not only society, culture, economic, and political order, but also morality, aesthetics, and the most intimate human experiences. According to Polish writer Jacek Dukaj (2019), who recently published a collection of essays called *After Writing*, the time has come to distinguish three epochs in human history: oral culture, literate culture, and postliterate culture, which involves the direct transfer of experiences (Dukaj, 2019, p. 209).[2]

Indeed, people across the world are being pushed with rising force into this postliterate world, where the written word as a medium to share thoughts and stories is gradually being replaced by direct transfers of experience and emotions through sounds, pictures, and moving images, recorded and shared with the use of multimedia technology. If this phenomenon is noticeable all around the globe, it appears particularly profound in the Chinese context, a culture uniquely bonded to writing. If, as Chris Hedges (2009) pointed out in *The Illusion of Literacy*, every society neglecting the competence and sensitivity developed through textual engagements is worrisome, then the ongoing shift from traditional *wen* 文 literacy in the Chinese context, towards (multi)media literacy, visual literacy, or transliteracy, is significantly problematic. Contemporary

[2] The term "postliteracy" appears as early as 1962, in Marshall McLuhan's *The Gutenberg Galaxy*.

China insists on continuity with its 'traditional culture' and unquestionably sees calligraphy and so-called ***hanzi wenhua*** 汉字文化 ('the culture of Chinese characters') as an important component of its current identity. If such continuity and identity are to be truly secured into the future, it is necessary to initiate a serious, comprehensive discussion concerning responsible shaping of the postliterate (though not scriptless) era, in which calligraphy may continue to play a major role and remain faithful to its spiritual roots.

## 4 Calligraphy and the Creative Industries

Calligraphy is a visual art and sustains connections with museums, galleries, and libraries. For centuries, calligraphy has also intersected in various ways with literature, music, performing arts, and design. More recently, it has found its way into fashion, advertising, branding, and architecture, both in China and abroad. In 1951, for instance, the world saw Christian Dior's playful cocktail dress "Quiproquo" (eng. "Misunderstanding") incorporating one of the most famous calligraphy pieces ever written in wild-cursive script—*Letter on a Stomach Ache* 肚痛帖 by Zhang Xu 张旭 (675–759) (Mair, 2015). In 2012, French architect Jean Nouvel won the competition for the design for the National Art Museum of China in Beijing, with a design in which the primary horizontal calligraphy stroke was transposed into the shape of the building. In 2015, renowned Chinese calligrapher Wang Dongling 王冬龄 was commissioned by the Apple Store to write Su Shi's 苏轼 poem *Drinking by the Lake: Clear Sky followed by Rain* 飲湖上初晴後雨 for the opening of their first store in Hangzhou. In 2018, Korean designer Chulan Kwak designed a modern chair and table that were inspired by Chinese cursive-brush writing, and in 2019, Thai designer Apiwat Chitapanya drew inspiration from the rhythm, movement, and flow of Chinese handwriting for her furniture series called *Ink Collection*. All of this speaks of the strong capacity of calligraphy to converge with creative industries even outside of art and museums, and suggests it may acquire new functions and meanings within the creative economy context, domestically and internationally.

Beyond boosting various national art and heritage-related industries, calligraphy as an art practice is also potentially a great resource for branding Chinese culture in China and abroad. Experiments linking certain aspects of calligraphy with new technologies, creative industries, or commercial culture indicate that calligraphy does not need to be as hermetic as it was for centuries, when it was accessible to and pursued only by a limited number of people in Chinese society. Noticeable in many contemporary promotional projects is the hope that calligraphy might enjoy a privileged position domestically and internationally; it can remain a source of national pride for Chinese people while actively contributing to China's economic growth and soft power. And yet, traditionally, there is another very different, but at least equally valid, understanding of calligraphy that is associated with continuous creative and spiritual endeavor, self-expression, and life practice. This poses a contradiction to attempts of superficial reproduction and wide distribution, which makes calligraphic culture available for the masses, but simultaneously dilutes its intrinsic value.[3] This aspect of calligraphy draws my scholarly attention, because it seems to be the most vulnerable to ongoing technological and social transformations in China.

Once calligraphy becomes perceived first and foremost as a creative force within the contemporary creative industries, seen primarily through the lens of cultural sectors, events, or brands, it will inevitably employ very different objectives and will develop along a very different trajectory (Miller, 2009). Rather than a practice capable of maintaining its own integrity and timeless strength, commercialization may transform calligraphy into something to be enhanced, transformed, or adjusted to the expectations of audiences. Objectives set by cultural policymakers, entrepreneurs, and managers may not necessarily prioritize the takeover of individual human content and transfer of complex skills. Market value is likely to gain importance over immeasurable things such as inspiration, education, self-growth, and intimate communication. In other words, there is a looming threat that, without enough caution, the common perception and experience of calligraphy will shift from a spiritual endeavor towards yet another branch of cultural consumption with local characteristics, becoming primarily accessible to mass audiences, visually pleasing and entertaining, and a means to generate an aura of cultural sophistication.

[3] Such concerns about the impacts of culture, such as promoting intellectual challenges to the arts, were voiced as early as 1947 by Theodor Adorno and Max Horkheimer in *Dialectic of Enlightenment*, most notably in a chapter entitled "The Culture Industry: Enlightenment as Mass Deception."

Though calligraphy was historically certainly also a form of leisure, it was leisure associated with intellectual and meditative pursuit. The question to be raised quite urgently—against the discourse of national pride, which reveals only part of the reality—is whether the majority of the Chinese practitioners engaging with calligraphy seeks opportunities to actively engage with brush practice or simply consume the products of this tradition within more or less imagined, short-lived 'events' and activities, able to generate more or less thrill and buzz on the social media, but soon forgotten. Back in 2017, a Chinese digital native informant, majoring in cultural management at a prestigious university, told me:

> All this engagement with traditional culture is just a fashion in China, not genuine cultural commitment or thorough revival. Currently we witness the craze for tradition and New Chinese Style, next will be AI and technology, and fad for smart furniture and AI-powered home appliances. (Interview, Shanghai, 2017)

She may have been exaggerating to an extent, but by now it is clear that she was onto something.

In his influential book, *Culture in a Liquid Modern World*, Zygmunt Bauman (2011) remarked on societies pushed to the edge where consumption becomes more valuable than tradition, where culture comes to consist "of offers, not prohibitions; propositions, not norms" (p. 13). Reflecting on Pierre Bourdieu's work on culture, Bauman (2011) suggested that "culture today is engaged in laying down temptations and setting up attractions, with luring and seducing, not with normative regulation; with PR rather than police supervision; with the production, sowing and planting of new needs and desires, rather than with duty" (ibid.). If calligraphy is successfully turned into a major creative industry, or into a major pillar supporting the expansion of other industries, it will have little chance to awaken and cultivate spiritual needs or artistic sensitivity. Rather, calligraphy will become a tool to enhance insatiable desires and increase consumption, and thus will end up contradicting itself.

Such contradictions already exist in each tacky gadget faking the presence of a sophisticated literati object, or each time a quick and cheap solution is applied to promote calligraphy, while everyone participating pretends not to notice the shoddiness of it. The contradiction exists each time technological reproductions of a calligraphy artwork are treated the same way as handwritten pieces.[4] Tragically, the contradiction exists when a monk offers a paper fan to a foreign female ink painting practitioner in Wuxi Plum Garden and says, "I wrote it," but the fan turns out to be only a poor resolution printout of his handwritten inscription 生歡喜心 ("Grow your inner happy heart"). The difference between a monk generously offering one of the relatively few inscriptions he has written himself as a souvenir of a meaningful encounter and a monk who had arranged in advance to get dozens of fans printed to be given away as promotion gifts in a photographable gesture of hospitality is exactly the difference between calligraphy perceived as a transformative life practice connecting humans and a cultural industry in the digital era.

Though there are certainly many artists, experts, and ordinary practitioners who continue to object to this trend of commercialism, and actively pursue calligraphy in relative seclusion as a life practice, how can we remain sure this new attitude will not become a significant threat? The ongoing shift from a model in which everyone who appreciated calligraphy and had interest in it could write it as well, towards appreciation, which does not necessarily require writing with the brush on a daily basis, tends to be already taken for granted. What will be the next compromise? Is it better to adopt the position of an optimist, or speak as a skeptic and point to worrisome trends? I choose to do the latter, and I insist that while calligraphy is a creative practice with the potential to nurture creative people and a cultured lifestyle, and thereby indirectly support growth in the creative and leisure industries in China, it should by all means be saved from becoming a distinct sector of creative industries or a commodity itself.

## 5 Digital W-r-i-t-i-n-g

Daily writing on keyboards and screens alienates people from handwritten words consisting of flowing lines and endlessly variable strokes. Characters look and feel completely different, depending on whether they appeared at once as a complete word unit (as a preexistent assemblage of constituent strokes), or whether they gradually emerged through a

[4] Here, I am not referring to Walter Benjamin's claim in *The Work of Art in the Age of Mechanical Reproduction* that reproduction damages the aura of the original. I simply mean to point out a diminishing awareness of certain crucial aspects of calligraphy: long-term commitment and handwriting.

sequence of movements. As Tim Ingold (2016) aptly noticed in relation to alphabetical scripts, "In the typed or printed text, every letter or punctuation mark is wrapped up in itself, totally detached from its neighbours to left and right" (p. 93). The same is true for characters. Moreover, the writing experience itself becomes significantly transformed when the writing person is switching from handwriting to the keyboard or digital text generators, which increasingly deprive the 'writer' of initial complex movement of the body, physical effort, and sensual experience (Ingold, 2016, pp. 26, 144). Who still remembers the original form and meaning of *shu* 书 (書)—a crucial character in the context of Chinese literacy—the raised human hand, which equipped with a writing tool directed vertically to the ground is used to move to write characters? Technology has transformed the very act of writing something down, allowing the people 'writing' on the screens to do so in any position, even while walking. Technology has also enabled transition from characters carefully integrated into imaginary squares, and written by hand, which moves across time and space, towards characters which are w-r-i-t-t-e-n on a stationary keyboard or acquired by finger or stylus through an adequate handwriting input program on the screen of an electronic device.

Chinese input software turns writing into an act of obtaining, recognizing, and selecting characters. Moreover, Chinese Pinyin input method editors (such like popular Sogou Pinyin) that rely on the use of Pinyin (i.e., the official system for the transcription of the standard Mandarin into the Latin alphabet) require users to refer to another script. This means that if I want to type in Chinese, I begin by typing a combination of Latin letters. I do not even have to mark the tones, because the device will suggest characters and words anyway, displaying them for me according to the frequency of their occurrence. It saves my time and in fact also cuts short the time I would have spent processing the content I intend to write, if I was handwriting. I quickly compare proposed characters, recognize them (sometimes just on the basis of one particularly characteristic graphic element), and accept the ones I need. The character *shu* 书 (書) does not emerge from a harmonized sequence of brush strokes; instead, it appears from the sequence of keys: s-h-u-space.

This process of 'writing' is pretty much the same for any Chinese or foreign person, unless they use another common system involving a 'handwriting' input software. In such case, the user writes more or less elegant combination of lines, which is quite a compromise between what technology can recognize and what the user intended to write on the screen, with the machine ultimately suggesting options of the most likely characters to choose from. This task can be easily fulfilled in the darkness, while lying on bed in a random position. Again, nothing of the initial writing position prevails. I once made an experiment of drawing on my smartphone screen a flimsy star out of three intersecting strokes. Despite the wrong proportions, as well as number and order of the strokes, the software still made an immediate bold attempt to recognize the character *yong* 永 in it ("forever, always"—quite ironically, the first character in calligraphy training, combining all main brushstrokes). In actual writing and calligraphy, this character would not appear well-balanced unless the writer managed to achieve, through extended time and patient practice, inner peace, a sure spiritual connection with sky and earth (both through the writing tool and the entire body). What seems particularly worth noticing is that after the right character has been selected, any trace of the initial individual tracing of the strokes by the user is gone, and a typed version of the character appears. It does not matter whether the person who 'wrote' on the surface of the smartphone screen was a famous calligrapher or a struggling barely literate person—in the blink of an eye both words become the same. Even digital handwriting is not allowed to last; it disappears replaced by perfectly legible and standardized 'writing,' easily processed by the machines.

Moving from handwriting and paper to keyboard and screen means abandoning specific psychophysical training. Writing characters by hand requires constant attentiveness and awareness of the position of fingers, back, elbow, and even the feet. It implies a comprehension of space, overall structure, and square areas from which everything in China begins, and which influences all aspects of Chinese culture, including its ideal of beauty. Now, the machine measures, counts, and composes text instantly on its own. As a result, the characters no longer belong to squares, but to the dense horizontal lines. The machine easily simulates evenness and clarity of thoughts—no matter how much the hands tremble as they hit the keyboard in a great hurry. It relieves the writer from the obligation of concentration and those arduous exercises that once made it possible to finally achieve correct character proportions and forms. Machine mediation equalizes the rhythm of writing, while also eliminating the differences in the internal dynamics of handwriting in different scripts. However, for instance, the fluency and internal consistency of my handwriting in various languages vary depending on how much writing I have done in each of them over the years; in digital reincarnations, they are all harmonized and equally neat.

Even though some devices and software features allow for saving digital handwriting in an unaltered form, the complex sensual experience is gone. Calligraphy is the opposite of a sterile screen too because it is a practice embedded in the physical world of speed, light, texture, wetness, and pressure. It is a multi-sensory experience. It involves ink and water transforming each other throughout the creative process. The ink has a smell, and the brush makes a quiet sound as it moves along the paper, which maintains its own textures, sounds, and presence and needs to be understood for the sake of obtaining desired visual effects.

Contemporary technologically mediated writing is not only deprived of these sensual components, but also of any trace of emotion. Moving from the standard writing routines of a contemporary Chinese city to the practice of calligraphy implies, among other things, stepping out of the reality in which even most personal writing—poetry, love messages, secret confessions—is technologically mediated. Here, feeling is conveyed by the choice of words, but not by the expressiveness of the lines and overall composition of those words (Ingold, 2016, p. 3). How does one switch smoothly from this approach to a calligraphy mindset, where the strokes themselves are able to register the deepest of tensions or sudden bursts of uncontrollable feeling? And how are we to encourage people to leave behind—at least for a while—the screen, which is tiring in its saturation of joy, excitement, uncertainty, entertainment, disappointment, stress, and fear? A screen that shows us everything it absorbs and generates throughout the day, that is used for writing as well as for all other tasks—receiving calls, taking photos, tracking packages and deliveries, arranging schedules, playing games, listening to music, reading, watching movies, reading news, interacting on social media? The paper, which I lay out in front of me during brush practice, does not aspire to be such a multi-functional tool, and it impacts the quality and integrity of thought and writing it quietly welcomes.

## 6 Simulating Calligraphy Practice

New technology not only draws people away from handwriting by transforming the very practice and perception of writing, but has also begun to offer experiences simulating Chinese calligraphy, replicating the visual effect of brush practice in a digital format. In this section, I discuss briefly

Zen Brush application, used by Chinese people and foreigners, either to add a bit of a 'brush feel' to the Chinese text, or to create visual content evoking Chinese aesthetic ambience. Many doubts and observations concerning particular features or the narrative surrounding this application apply to other similar tools available in the market as well, but I chose to focus on Zen Brush, because I am most familiar with it.

According to its official description, Zen Brush focuses on "the strong yet beautiful feel of the East Asian ink brush" (Apple, 2020) and allows one to save their work as a shareable picture. Currently, a third iteration of this application is available, under the name Zen Brush 3. Using a finger or a tool such as the Apple Pencil or Surface Pen, the app allows both writing and drawing, and the intuitive user interface is said to be "imbued with the Zen spirit" and "optimal for performing Zen art" (PSOFT, 2022b). Users can choose from a great variety of background templates, which are digital equivalents of textured craft paper, or 3D objects used in calligraphy, like paper fans. Creators, salespeople, and users praise Zen Brush as a realistic ink painting simulation that reproduces the delicate and vivid strokes of an ink brush. The app description mentions such crucial qualities and features as "providing a sensation just like a real ink brush," a chance to "enjoy the complex, three-dimensional expressiveness of ink-wash painting where the ink gradually soaks into washi (Japanese paper)" or "ability to adjust the thickness of the ink" (PSOFT, 2022a). In addition, the user has at their disposal two features: 'eraser brush' and 'undo/redo,' options unheard of in the long traditions of both Chinese and Japanese calligraphy, which consider written strokes as definite and unmodifiable. One of the main improvements in version 3 of Zen Brush was adding an option to adjust 'amount of water', and according to one of the websites, it is now "more brush-like than a real brush" (PSOFT, 2022b).

I do not intend to evaluate this app in terms of potential it creates for visual artists and designers, or its capacity to help Chinese language students memorize the strokes and entire characters by keeping them entertained. Or even its validity as yet another joyful pastime involving the screen. However, for the sake of preserving calligraphy's spiritual and physical core (involving the cautiously breathing and acting human body), I want to insist once more on distinguishing decisively between the digital brush (电子毛笔), which is able to create digital calligraphy or ink painting, and the actual soft Chinese brush (毛笔), which does not allow one to undo a single line, but allows a skillful practitioner to develop endless layers of subtle shades in ink that imply a multitude of colors without representing them individually (墨分五色) (Hung, 2012).

Another application worthy of attention in the given context is Live Calligraphy, an app which promises that by practicing Chinese brush calligraphy with your finger (which should be more accurately depicted as simply obtaining Chinese characters on the screen with the finger tracing provided samples) "you can feel yourself like a real master of Chinese calligraphy, and fully enjoy the artistic charm of the art of calligraphy" (Sheng). It should be decisively stated that it is an illusion that practitioners perform the 'writing.' The elegant characters appear on the screen as a result of the great competence of the designers and programmers who created the application, not the 'writer.' Those who claim that the digital experience of a forgiving, clean, and entirely nonexistent brush is the same, or exceeds the real brush experience, have only insufficient exposure to the complex and generous writing instrument, which true brush practitioners may struggle to fully comprehend and master over their entire lives.

While it is tempting to claim that such apps could facilitate more regular calligraphy engagement among young people because they do not require preparation of paper and ink, this is a myth. In fact, genuine calligraphy practitioners who realize the core energy and handwriting aspect of this pursuit, but experience difficulty in practicing it in regular format on a regular basis, tend to resort to other solutions—pen calligraphy (硬笔书法) or writing with a brush on water paper scroll. Smartphones or iPads used for practice are at best used to display copied works of Ouyang Xun 欧阳询 or Huaisu 懷素. Unlike the 'practicing' on digital applications, writing with water on the so-called magic paper allows a practitioner to maintain the complexity in the movement of the body, arm, or hand.

Running a finger across the screen shall not be considered a calligraphic gesture because it has nothing in common with it. Apps like Live Calligraphy that fake the perfect shapes of characters, as if the user was as skilled as one of the most renowned calligraphers of all times, Wang Xizhi 王羲之, are harmful in the sense that they actively distort perception of the competence and effort required in calligraphy. It all appears seamless, light, and painless whereas, in reality, it requires incredible commitment and tireless work.

An expressive brush captured in action in the Zen Brush app's icon is, in fact, only a bitter reminiscence of the absent brush, which had been abandoned for the sake of a digital toy. It does not constitute an attempt to harmonize calligraphy tradition with digital writing. It is simply a skeuomorphism—a recreation of the former shape and an imitation of old materials in new technology and surroundings. Marcin Wicha (2018) warned that using old shapes is always meant to calm the user down. He wrote, "Everything is the old way. It is still your world, you can find yourself in it. Just do what needs to be done. We will take care of the rest" (Wicha, 2018, p. 82). Indeed, skeuomorphism puts vigilance to sleep and simulates a lasting friendly world, even though in this supposedly familiar world, despite all the marking of calligraphy's omnipresence and its supposed unthreatened continuity, it is getting harder and harder to find actual calligraphy and write it. Rather, this is a world abundant in fonts and graphic designs that mimic calligraphic shapes and layouts. A world in which digital calligraphy generators can customize any content with Mao Zedong's 毛泽东 calligraphy style for anyone, even though relatively few people are able to copy his handwriting with a brush (Bandurski, 2019).[5] As a result, it is also a world which urgently requires systematic reflection on how to act in the long run, in order to preserve an internally diverse writing ecosystem, in which calligraphy could remain alive and evolve according to its own logic and dynamics.

To maintain the spirit, strength, and core values of calligraphy throughout the current challenges, it is desirable to seek a path not away from the technological transformation—as if pretending it is not happening and cannot harm calligraphy—but beyond it. In my approach, I do not stand against modernization, technological development, the evolution of tradition, or digital calligraphy as such. I do, however, stand firmly against the pretense that a practice to which brush, ink, water, paper, and human being are central remains the same after any of the components had been removed or replaced. Sometimes, at scholarly or art events related to technology and creative industries, I encounter people fantasizing that one day humanity will be able to read back into renowned masters' emotions and minds. In these moments, I am concerned that, were such a trajectory of unconstrained technological experimentation to become dominant in modernizing China, we would inevitably arrive at a dead end. I fear that one day we may indeed end up in Dong Qichang's 董其昌 or Hong Yi's 弘一 heads, but we will not be able to distinguish their brushstroke from others, we won't be able to read what their scrolls

[5] Font converter website: 毛体字体转换器在线生成器, http://www.diyiziti.com/Builder/308.

say, and we will neither feel the desire, nor have the capability, to write anything of our own. The necessary capabilities to relieve this tension, this fear, are realized by all those people who, despite all the technological intrusion in daily urban life, nevertheless patiently stick to their soft brushes and practice.

## 7 Robotic Arm with a Brush

In the previous section, I briefly touched on the digital 'calligraphy experience,' in which a human being supposedly engages with the ink brush, though neither a brush nor paper are anywhere to be seen. A flipside of such a situation is that in which some form of calligraphy, written with the brush and ink, appears on a tangible piece of paper, though a human through whose body the *qi* 气 could flow is nowhere to be seen: characters written by a robotic arm. Emerging robotic calligraphy constitutes a fascinating new chapter in the history of script-driven distinction between the Self and the Other, between own and alien, between barbarians and civilization, which throughout the centuries were made by Chinese people based on one's ability to write and read Chinese characters.

A short shot of a robotic arm writing with a brush in Chinese and in English was incorporated into the 2021 China International Import Expo promotion video, which circulated widely online and spread a message of China's openness and readiness to welcome the world.[6] In a way, it seemed like another twist on the fantasy of calligraphy written by a non-human being, which can be dated back at least to the Jaquet-Droz clock featuring a kneeling young writer in Georgian court suits who uses a brush pen to write in Chinese. It was one of the Qianlong Emperor's favorite timepieces and it remained on display in the Forbidden City during my last visit. The automaton writes vertically, a text of 8 characters: 八方向化, 九土来王, meaning "neighboring countries are looking forward to visiting the highly civilized empire; all people in the world should come to respect and tribute its emperor" (Wang, 2020).

Contemporary technological advancement, pursued in different countries, has reached new frontiers in transposing this complex writing skill to a non-human. Back in 2012, a research group at Keio University, led by Seiichiro Katsura, has developed the Motion Copy System. Japanese

[6] This video can be watched at: https://www.bilibili.com/video/BV18U4y1g7YF?from=search&seid=12792627261617641821&spm_id_from=333.337.0.0.

scientists developed a robot that can learn the inclination and shape of the brush, recording the force and sensation of a human being's touch as digital data. This means that robots are gradually gaining access to skill content and reproducing not only calligraphic works but also the movements of a living calligrapher. In other words, robots are beginning to write using gestures similar to humans, and the human task in such endeavor is to figure out the brushstrokes that the machine should apprehend. Questions arise regarding the distinction between programmed writing and artistic writing, as well as the importance of possessing a heart and emotions in order to create true brushworks (Interview with Pan Jianfeng, Shanghai, April 2021). Can a being without feelings become a brush practitioner, or will that writing be inevitably empty and dead? Robots may be trained to control the motion of the brush, but can they be taught free expression? Part of the intrinsic beauty of calligraphy is that two characters written by the same hand even immediately one after another will never look and feel the same. How can this quality be transposed in robotic writing? Would anyone actually dare to program 'unpredictable effects,' or integrate possibility of a 'beautiful imperfection' in such an advanced technology?

Interestingly, robots have been already designed for tea ceremony, as well as playing Chinese abstract strategy board game Weiqi and Chinese Zither. It is too early to know whether this will indeed become a significant trend, but already these robots invite inquiry around whether it makes sense to assign the responsibility of maintaining human cultural continuity to someone/something else. More specifically, the most significant query to me in this context is whether the objective is to produce a sound, pour the tea, (re)write the characters, or, perhaps, as in the past, cultivate the individual personality and graciousness of a human in the process? Was it not the act of creation and sharing, and the continuous aim towards perfection, that remained central to each of these traditional practices? Are we to believe that such a merging of ethics with aesthetics can be performed equally well by robots? I am aware that currently, for a single robot there are still thousands of people practicing handwriting with ink and brush and pouring tea from crafted teapots into favorite handmade teacups; yet all my doubts remain.

The Shanghai Science and Technology Museum takes pride in its section themed "The Development and Application of Robotics," which displays robots that are able to draw portraits of the visitors, solve Rubik cubes, and perform synchronized dances. In 2014, Chinese President

Xi Jinping 习近平 called for a "robot revolution" in order to elevate China's manufacturing capabilities, boost productivity, and counteract the consequences of the demographic crisis (Bateman, 2018). Last year, Mayor of Beijing Chen Jining 陈吉宁 announced, "The robot industry is one of the major priorities in Beijing's accelerating process to become an international sci-tech innovation center" (Aisyah, 2021). In my view, such a statement emphasizes the need for reflection on the reasons and possible outcomes of engaging robots with calligraphy at this relatively early stage.[7]

How do we define the core value of brush practice? Is it about the beauty of created characters, or first of all about the human experience that enables a calligraphy piece to emerge? In an effort to make this issue even more clear, we may inquire in a slightly exaggerated mood, whether anyone actually believes it possible to maintain calligraphy predominantly via robots. After all, what does it actually mean to say 'robot mastered Chinese calligraphy'? That it can provide a high-quality copy of a piece created and provided by a human? What will it reveal about shifting understandings of the human and calligraphy if we begin to validate a mindset in which merely a productive arm is enough to maintain brush practice? Why assign the task of writing a beautiful character to technology, as if it was equal to cleaning laundry, or collecting geological samples, or mass producing an ornament in a factory? Again, what is the ultimate goal and purpose: to have a beautifully written character or to cultivate skill and temperament?

The key point for me here is not to decide whether what robots 'write' or 'copy' can be considered calligraphy, or whether at some point in the future robots may become able to create a highly expressive calligraphy piece. Neither am I concerned with questions about whether it is or will be possible for people in the nearest future to distinguish between human and robotic brushwork. I want however to point out the importance of reflection what is the purpose of such robotic copying. After

[7] A controversy that triggered a broader conversation about the purpose and value of handwriting was caused in 2019 by a young student who secretly used a 'handwriting robot' to complete her handwriting assignments faster. Such robots, able to mimic the handwriting of the writer, are already quite easily available for purchase in China, which seems to be yet more proof that Chinese society may be gradually heading towards another large-scale revolution concerning its writing (Daniel Victor and Tiffany May, *Chinese Girl Finds a Way Out of Tedious Homework: Make a Robot Do It*, https://www.nytimes.com/2019/02/21/world/asia/china-handwriting-robot.html).

all, according to literati tradition, copying calligraphy texts or paintings was a complex artistic and spiritual endeavor. The main objective was to shape one's mind and personality through practice, and not to get an extra copy of a particular scroll or album leaf. The main concern was to have more humans acquire particular skills and sensitivity in preparation for their own meaningful creation, and not to produce another perfect copy of an existing piece. How much of robotic calligraphy is about pushing calligraphy to a new experimental stage? How much is about exploring possibilities to customize massively produced texts? And how much is it simply about storing diminishing manual skills on computers, so that they can be made available on a network when necessary?

I acknowledge that art created by AI can be genuinely touching, and that in fact more and more of human culture and art is already being created with some level of AI participation (Dukaj, 2019, p. 124). I am also aware that, as Jacek Dukaj (2019) aptly noted, practically "no work of art that requires a budget that exceeds the capabilities of the individual is no longer solely man-made" (p. 125). However, calligraphy cannot exceed the financial capabilities of the practicing individual. Anyone able to afford basic utensils and to allocate time for practice in their schedule can engage in this practice. Why, then, make such a persistent effort to entangle calligraphy with AI and other forms of technology? Why is it that one of the relatively few remaining practices that require one to disconnect from the digital and virtual surroundings and enhance own integrity, should be requested to subjugate to technology as well? What priorities, aspirations, and ambitions support such efforts? What matters to me here in particular is the reasoning and meaning of such endeavors defined from a human perspective. From the perspective of human society, which is already unquestionably transformed and reformed by technology, the facilitation of access to digital content works to disconnect humans from one another. This occurs partly through an increased exposure to film, gaming, and advertising industries, all generated and distributed with profound use of AI and digital technologies, which are now turning to transform calligraphy as well.

## 8 Concluding Remarks

Speaking as cultural historian and anthropologist, in this chapter I began an investigation into the entanglement of handwriting and technology in contemporary China, and the implications this has for Chinese brush writing. My reflection figures calligraphy within the changing urban environment and aboard the ongoing transition towards a postliterate era. In light of the dominant writing and typing practices of the digital era, I have uncovered potential implications for traditional handwriting, particularly regarding the outcomes of two significant emerging trends—applications simulating calligraphy experience on the screen and robotic calligraphy. By doing so, I intend to highlight the impact of technology on the Chinese people's relationship with one of the most revered creative practices in Chinese cultural heritage at large. At this point, though I have more questions than decisive answers, posing such questions seems highly valuable in instigating a broader debate about the prospects of writing practices and cultures of literacy in the postliterate world. It is noteworthy that Chinese culture has, at its core, both a writing practice and an art practice. What will be the implications in a contemporary world, which does not maintain the same relationship to either the (handwritten) word, which is rapidly overtaken by the new technologies, or art, which is increasingly molded to comply with requirements of consumerist culture? What if China shifts towards justifying the value and presence of these practices in terms of current market value, as opposed to their traditional values that transcend time and space?

According to my understanding, if Chinese brush practice is to be reimagined, but not reinvented as an entirely new visual phenomenon and creative practice for the contemporary world, the role of technology must be reimagined. At that point, responsible use of new technologies must be pursued in ways that maintain the multidimensionality and integrity of the practice, which has evolved from an imperial past into current era. The challenge is to strike a wise balance between technological innovation, attractive application, and accurate cultural content. Furthermore, it seems necessary to refrain from reducing calligraphy in the contemporary urban context to symbolic flows of ink, immersive digital illusions, casual art consumption, or random, short-lived thrills. There is a major difference between tapping into calligraphy for inspiration in a contemporary creative endeavor, preserving ink painting and calligraphy heritage for further study or appreciation, developing digital equivalents of this practice and heritage, and ensuring the continuity of calligraphy as a handwriting practice. Indeed, calligraphy is still actively pursued by some people, and therefore not dead. If at this point we fail to recognize these differences, and remain unable to secure a space for brush practice to grow organically from its old and twisted—but still vital—root, it will be lost.

As much as technology itself need not be a decisive threat itself, at times it is quite possible to imagine a dystopian future in which nobody is able anymore to truly engage with vanishing traditional culture, and all that is left are mesmerizing special effects and conspicuous consumption. However, it is still possible to insist on the real, living presence of calligraphy, and nurture genuine engagements with it so that such a dystopian future does not become reality. The skeptical assumption that advancing technology will destroy calligraphy does not have to be a self-fulfilling prophecy. On the contrary, the overwhelming presence of new technologies may be a great opportunity for a calligraphy revival. Brush practice involving ink may actually be seen as an opportunity for healing, and as such, it may have a vital role to play in helping people to reconnect with themselves, to reclaim meaningful communication with other people, and to seek emotional balance between their career and personal life. With minimal necessary requirements, this practice can provide a priceless space of mental reclusion to replenish creativity, concentration, kindness, and mindful presence. Furthermore, in a way, calligraphy offers a route into a parallel reality—a thrilling analogue world which values space, slowness, and humbleness rather than excess.

It is most certainly a delusion that calligraphy will be easily and mindlessly carried on into a world now determined by ambitions of the rapidly growing tech sector; into an era where machine-generated content increasingly challenges human content. Therefore, while persistently underlining the long history of calligraphy in China, a conversation about its future is much needed. Such a future cannot be defined merely as an investable engagement with technology, but must entail a bold vision beyond the current frame of cyberculture. We must pose daring inquiries about how and what of the brush legacy is to be sustained within the next fifty, hundred, or two hundred years.

Perhaps securing a space for calligraphy to grow in the global metropolis, amid digital transformation, should begin by noticing a societal shift from writing with a hand, to which soft brush was an extension, towards a smartphone as an almost permanent extension of people's bodies. For so many people, one hand is almost constantly blocked by a smartphone (sometimes even two smartphones), which even when not in use remains constantly at one's fingertips. The human hand becomes increasingly associated with *shouji* 手机 (mobile phone) not *shouji* 手

迹 (someone's original handwriting). The conceptual exercise enhancing the attempt to revive calligraphy may be to act towards an imagined world in which people are relying on their brushes the way they now depend on their phones—to keep the track of their lives, views, feelings, poems, inspirations, festive moments, and travels. The ultimate challenge in reintroducing calligraphy seems to be to overcome our coupling with technology in favor of a simple, but powerful tool that enables serene writing, and thereby nurtures crucial human capacity to cope with complexity and separate illusion from reality.

## References

Adorno, T., & Horkheimer, M. (1947). *Dialectic of enlightenment*. Querido.

Aisyah, K. (2021, September 17). *Robot Industry Shines in China*. https://opengovasia.com/robot-industry-shines-in-china/

Apple. (2020). *Zen Brush 3. Freely draw beautiful Zen art*. https://apps.apple.com/us/app/zen-brush-3/id1531841731

Bandurski, D. (2019, January 6). *Keeping to the Script*. https://chinamediaproject.org/2019/01/06/keeping-to-the-script/

Barrass, G. S. (2002). *The art of calligraphy in modern China*. University of California Press.

Bateman, J. (2018, June 22). *Why China is spending billions to develop an army of robots to turbocharge its economy*. CNBC. https://www.cnbc.com/2018/06/22/chinas-developing-an-army-of-robots-to-reboot-its-economy.html

Bauman, Z. (2011). *Culture in a liquid modern world*. Polity.

Ch'ien, E. N.-M. (2008). Symbolic revolutions. Xu Bing and his language art. *Wasafiri*, *23*, 56–67.

Dukaj, J. (2019). *Po piśmie*. Literackie.

Gernet, J. (2008). *Inteligencja Chin. Społeczeństwo i mentalność*. Wydawnictwo Fu Kang.

Hedges, C. (2009). *Empire of illusion: The end of literacy and the triumph of spectacle*. Bold Type Books.

Hung, W. (2012). *Variations of ink: A dialogue with Zhang Yanyuan*. https://lucian.uchicago.edu/blogs/wuhung/files/2012/12/Variations-of-Ink-A-Dialogue-with-Zhang-Yanyuan.pdf

Ingold, T. (2016). *Lines: A brief history*. Routledge.

Keane, M. (2013). *Creative industries in China: Art, design and media*. Polity.

Keane, M. (2021, October 18). *Digital Civilisation in the Making (Part 2)*. https://michael-keane.com/2021/10/18/digital-civilisation-in-the-making-part-2/

Lee, L. O.-F. (1999). *Shanghai modern: The flowering of a new urban culture in China, 1930–1945*. Harvard University Press.

Lindqvist, C. (2008). *China: Empire of living symbols*. Da Capo Press.

Mair, V. (2015). *Christian Dior's "Quiproquo" cocktail dress and the florid rhubarb prescription written on it*. https://languagelog.ldc.upenn.edu/nll/?p=19331

McLuhan, M. (1962). *The Gutenberg Galaxy: The making of typographic man*. University of Toronto Press.

Miller, T. (2009). From creative to cultural industries: Not all industries are cultural, and no industries are creative. *Cultural Studies, 23*(1), 88–99.

PSOFT. (2022a). *Zen Brush 2. Simple ink brush tool*. https://psoftmobile.net/en/zenbrush2-win.html

PSOFT. (2022b). *Zen Brush 3. Simple ink brush tool*. https://psoftmobile.net/en/zenbrush3.html

UNESCO. (2009). Article 8: Chinese Calligraphy. *Representative List of the Intangible Cultural Heritage of Humanity 2009*. https://ich.unesco.org/doc/src/06859-EN.pdf

Victor, D., & May, T. (2019). *Chinese girl finds a way out of tedious homework: Make a robot do it*. https://www.nytimes.com/2019/02/21/world/asia/china-handwriting-robot.html

Wang, S. (2020). *Luxury Timepieces—Key to the Gates of the Eastern Empire (Pt. 2)*. https://www.thehourglass.com/cultural-perspectives/luxury-timepieces-key-to-the-gates-of-the-eastern-empire-pt-2/

Wicha, M. (2018). *Jak przestałem kochać design*. Karakter.

Yen, Y. (2005). *Calligraphy and power in contemporary Chinese society*. Routledge.

Zheng, D. (1994). Chinese calligraphy and the Cultural Revolution. *Journal of Popular Culture, 28*(2, Fall), 185–201.

CHAPTER 3

# From Rehabilitated Factories to Cyberspace: The Migration of the Art Ecosystem in Shanghai

*Alexandre Ouairy*

## 1 Introduction

At the turn of the 2000s, the Shanghai municipal government aimed to make the city a global creative center. It launched a series of policies that economically transformed the city. This period initiated the emergence of the creative industries and the city's first creative clusters, with artists and their art playing a significant role. However, the government's top-down approach entailed the creation and installation of institutions to regulate this development, with these government bodies necessitating ever-growing investments in and financialization of the art ecosystem. These regulations triggered a complex relationship between

A. Ouairy (✉)
Department of History of Art and Archaeology, SOAS University of London, London, UK
e-mail: Alexandre_Ouairy@soas.ac.uk



S. Chrétien-Ichikawa and K. Pawlik (eds.), *Creative Industries and Digital Transformation in China*,
https://doi.org/10.1007/978-981-19-3049-2_3

the government, the market, and artists, leading to the development of art ecologies. Moreover, Shanghai's urban transformation dramatically affected the artists' position within the city, which shifted to favor other commercial creative industries such as design and advertising agencies. The process accelerated artists' exploration of new territories and their adoption of the Internet into their art practice. These shifts profoundly changed the way artists negotiated and produced art forms in Shanghai.

To give an account of the transformation of Shanghai's contemporary art ecosystem, it is necessary to review the birth and evolution of art communities after the Opening Reforms, an economic program launched in 1979 by Deng Xiaoping that dramatically transformed the society. Known as "Socialism with Chinese characteristics," the reforms aimed at modernizing the economy while initiating the rapid economic growth that characterized early twenty-first-century China. The reforms gradually moved away from state-ownership and the planned market economy. First, the reforms deregulated pricing and lifted some protectionist policies, which opened the market to entrepreneurship and foreign investments. It then aimed at privatizing state-owned enterprises. The implementation of the policies accelerated in 1992, after a series of speeches that Deng Xiaoping pronounced during his visit to China's southern cities (Shenzhen, Zhuhai, Guangdong, and Shanghai), where he reinforced the importance of the reforms.

In addition to its implications for the economy at large, the Opening Reforms meant less state control over creative production. It allowed the possibility for artists to disengage from official programs to develop their own independent creations. Artists moved away from strict Socialist Realism styles depicting Communist values and an idealized society, and started to embrace global artistic languages and different approaches to subjectivity that were emerging in the late 1970s. While many artistic works were broadly mediated with a modernist influence, many other works relied on words and signs to openly rebel against the authority of both state ideology and the institutional apparatus of art as represented by academia, traditionalists, and party bureaucrats. Some other creations experimented with performances.

However, in the early 1980s, independent artistic institutions did not exist in China and exhibitions were not permitted outside of state-authorized spaces (Gao, 2012). To operate autonomously, artists organized themselves in groups such as Caocao, Stars Group, and New Wave 85. These associations provided the economic support necessary to organize exhibitions, as well as creating an initial framework where practices were negotiated, and to limit individual risk (Salmenkari, 2004). Artists often managed to elude both the control of the authorities and the exhibition organizers through participating in these groups. Subsequently, many exhibitions, such as "China/Avant-Garde" presented at the China Art Gallery in Beijing (now the National Art Museum of China) in 1989, resulted in shows' temporary suspensions (DeBevoise, 2014). Up to 1989, art in China was marked by small-scale paintings and experimentation reserved for a small community of enthusiasts but not yet actively collected. However, after the students' demonstration in Tiananmen Square and the subsequent repression of 1989, unauthorized activities in public exhibition spaces were officially banned and many groups had to quickly disband. Artists then organized exhibitions only in private spaces, inaugurating what came to be called "Apartment Art" (Gao, 2003).

While art production in post-reforms China resembled other post-socialist countries in certain respects, the influence of reforms was minimized in comparison (Erjavec & Groïs, 2003). The nascent artistic institutional framework was still overshadowed by the political apparatus, and experimentation toward creative freedom quickly disbanded in 1989. In the mid-1990s, artists moved from the confinement of their home to the remains of the city's industrial past; commercial galleries emerged, which led art from China to gain recognition both locally and internationally. These changes in the 1990s launched the creative industries.

## 2 Shanghai's First Creative Cluster and the Art Market Boom

The acceleration of the economic reforms and the privatization of state-owned companies in the early 1990s transformed China's cities. Municipalities like Shanghai restructured their urban fabric and delocalized high energy-consuming and polluting industry sites from the city center. The ambition of the municipality to make Shanghai a global city accelerated the decline of the manufacturing sector. The city further encouraged former manufacturers to refurbish and lease space to "urban industries." One key example is the case of the site now known as M50, a textile factory owned by Shangtex group, situated on Moganshan Road no. 50 on the bank of the Suzhou River in downtown Shanghai. The textile group was required to downsize, before closing the site entirely at the turn of the century (Sheng, 2011). M50 become the first creative cluster in Shanghai, and the warehouses offered large studios to artists at a low cost. In 1999, about 50 buildings in various industrial architectural styles from the 1930s to the 1990s became available in the factory complex, covering 40,000 square meters.

Artists were among the first to move in. However, the government was still dubious of the intentions of the artists after the artistic experiences of the early 1980s. Furthermore, art studios were not listed as official "urban industries," a designation that encouraged the city to lease state-owned enterprises to businesses. The complex's management, therefore, took the risk of allowing artists to rent studio space in an industrial zone (Sheng, 2011). However, the strategy eventually became crucial in revitalizing the industrial character of the city and growing a prominent art district. Indeed, after some prominent artists, including Xue Song, Xu Zhen, and Ding Yi, installed their studios there or in the vicinity, art galleries located there as well.

Shanghart Gallery was among the first to transform M50's disused industrial space into an art district. The gallery was the first commercial art space in Shanghai when Lorenz Helbling opened it in 1996 in the corridor of the Portman Hotel (now the Portman Ritz-Carlton) on Nanjing Road. Through the years, it became one of the most important institutions in the promotion of contemporary art from China. Helbling later moved Shanghart into its own space next to Fuxing Park. Finally, in 2000, the gallery settled down in M50, where it still has a space to this today (Sheng, 2011). After Helbling's success, other galleries burgeoned at M50, including Eastlink Gallery, Pantocrator, Island 6, and Studio Rouge, to name but a few. Davide Quadrio established the base for Bizart, Shanghai's first non-profit art organization, in M50. Finally, some artists opened small cafés, where they met for chats with visitors and art patrons. The mix of artist studios with commercial and non-commercial spaces marked the beginning of a new art ecology in Shanghai.

The creative cluster accelerated the commercialization of contemporary art from China. International organizations such as the British Council, as well as and foreign artists, visited and established connections between M50's community and the global artistic network (Gu, 2012). These exchanges extended beyond traditional art forms and allowed foreign advertising agencies to make links to fashion, branding events, performance photography, and music, all while participating in the international identity of M50. While the site was mostly unknown to local audiences, the site transformed into a catalyst to attract international collectors (Gu, 2012). The cluster combined production in the artists' studios, exhibitions, and sales of the work in gallery spaces. The same year that Shanghart settled in M50, it participated in the prestigious Basel art fair, a first for a Chinese gallery. It marked a milestone in the recognition and commercial success of art from China.

The international success of art production from China coincides with the Political Pop and Cynical Realism movements. These artistic trends, coined by Li Xianting in 1992, drew on the immediacy of the artist's personal experiences in post-socialist China (Poplin, 2017). Works of the period are exemplified by a reference to the socialist past mixed with images of international brands and the exploration of subjectivities in the new market-driven economic environment. The works captured the ongoing interactions between the state and the market, in the influence and control of art production in the years to come (DeBevoise, 2014). In answer to the growing demand from the art market, artists developed a new strategy for systematic production: the series. Figures of the Political Pop movement, such as Wang Guangyi, rode the wave of this success. He started the Great Criticism series in 1990 and continued it until 2007 (Erjavec & Groïs, 2003). The paintings are mostly made of four solid colors: red, yellow, gray, and white. Compositions follow a general principle: socialist propaganda poster-inspired figures that rest against a plain red background. In the background is a white logo of foreign brands and a series of random serial numbers. Although Sotheby records more than 250 works from the Great Criticism series, the artists decided to halt the series in 2007. As Wang Guangyi mentioned:

> The paintings were meant to show that although the two systems, the political and the commercial, are not united—and are even in conflict—the principal goal of each is to convince the population at large of the authenticity and singularity of its products in modern Chinese society. (Erjavec & Groïs, 2003, p. 255)

Major representatives of Cynical Realism followed a similar strategy of seriality and systemic construction. For instance, Zhang Xiaogang's *Bloodline* series started in 1993 and continued until 2011. Most works are characterized by gray backgrounds with predominantly monochromatic human figures. Unexpressive and frontal, wearing an outfit reminiscent of the Maoist uniform, the figures in the series recall Chinese family portraits of the 1950s. A thin red line links the different figures. As Zhang (2017) told the *South China Morning Post*:

> I tried doing other things after 1998, but the exhibitions' demand for the series left me little time. By 2000, I wanted to cut down on my output, but it was very hard after the market took off. It is very difficult for my generation of artists to say no to patrons. (p. 6)

To accommodate the market, some artists calculated prices based on the square meters of the artworks.

The commercial success of contemporary art accelerated the gentrification of M50. By the mid-2000s, Chinese contemporary art attracted mainstream attention. National and foreign media covered the creative cluster, as they would also do for Beijing's 798 art district. The publicity was less about the art than about the cluster phenomenon (Gu, 2012). As a result, M50 quickly became a tourist destination that also attracted other creative industries, namely design agencies and architecture studios. The site management company slowly increased the rent prices, driving working artists away. Ironically, M50 is now officially registered as an "art center" tourist landmark while marketing agencies, fashion boutiques, and cafés have replaced many of the artist studios, and some of the initial art galleries. The artists helped in building M50's creative image yet have been replaced by other commercial output.

After M50, Shangtex, the holding group managing the cluster, refurbished several other industrial sites on the outskirts of the city. Two in particular are relevant in exploring the Shangtex strategy of reconversion. The first one, nicknamed M50 Taopu by some artists, is located at Wuwei Road No. 18. Newly renovated, the managing group offered favorable conditions to artists and galleries to settle there. In 2010, Shanghart installed the first warehouse-type museum on that site. The second cluster, situated at 18 Linqing Road in Yangpu District, hosted Magda Danyz's gallery. The managing group hoped that art galleries and the presence of artists would accelerate both the promotion and rental of these spaces. However, it did not necessarily envision the success it faced. Ultimately, prices were still too high for artists, and public transportation access was limited.

## 3 Alternative Space, Self-Organization, and Artists as Agents of Gentrification

While commercial success helped certain artists rise to stardom, groups of emerging artists looked for alternatives to M50's increasing rent prices. Taking inspiration from Shanghai's original art cluster, they look for other disused sites. In 2006, some artists settled right in the heart of the city's Jing'an District, at 696 Weihai Road, a few blocks away from the luxury shopping mall Plaza 66. At the time, the site was under the jurisdiction of the Chinese Communist Party (CCP) secretary of Shanghai and became available after he was accused of corruption. At the margin of the already established art market, Weihai 669 mixed local and international emerging artists with bohemian inspirations. Weihai 696 became Shanghai's center of art and a hub for transnational creative types (Zhou, 2015). For a while, as Zhou Ying recalls, Weihai 696 remained the only place in downtown Shanghai outside the formality of administrative prescription, with low rents, organic structures, and an informal atmosphere (Zhou, 2015). The space offers a place for eclectic forms and artistic freedom. While many artists used painting as their primary medium, others experimented with photographs, installations, multimedia works, and performances. This space's artistic production contrasted with the commercial output of M50. Art at Weihai 696 was shown during open-studio sessions and drew a larger crowd on the weekends, mixing spontaneous art performances, barbecues, and improvised parties.

However, like Moganshan Road, the Weihai site quickly became an entertainment destination. As the number of official creative clusters rose along with rental prices, the future of Weihai 696 followed the path of M50. In 2004, the Economic Council established the Shanghai Creative Industry Center (SCIC), which allowed 18 sites to be designated as creative clusters by 2005, including M50. By 2006, this number grew to 85 (Zhou, 2015). By 2011, none of the tenants of Weihai 696 was able to renew their lease, leading the site to shut down and artists to be evicted. After years of speculation about the site's next reconversion, in 2017 WeWork unveiled its flagship co-working space for creative industries at that location. It marked the New York start-up's expansion into China in partnership with property management company Sino-Ocean Group. On its website, WeWork introduces Weihai 696 as:

> [a] historical London style mansion [that] once was home to more than 40 artist studios and galleries. Today, the building has transformed into a modern workspace, which attracts not just artists, but aspiring entrepreneurs, designers and emerging businesses large and small. (Zhou, 2015)

Due to these developments, no artists are present in the current facilities, as high rent prices, fancy interior design, and open space do not easily accommodate artists' studio practices.

Following the dismantling of Weihai Road, in 2012 some of the artists move to Liyang Road 111, in Hongkou District. The venue had already been refurbished. Though the rent was kept relatively low to accommodate artists, the future of the studio was uncertain, given so many failures of collective artistic spaces in the previous years. Not long after moving in, the rents were raised, and artists had to migrate further away to the suburbs, including some that moved to the former Hero Pen factory in Taopu, not far from Shangtex's project. Already, real estate developers' usage of art as a promotional and gentrification accelerator became common practice, though success in their individual endeavors has varied.

Indeed, for almost three decades, the model of urban redevelopment in Shanghai has been large-scale demolition, reconstruction, and resettlement. Billions of square meters of old houses have been demolished and replaced by new buildings. With the disappearance of former neighborhoods, millions of local residents have been displaced (Zhong & Chen, 2017). The massive urban transformation in the process of making Shanghai a leading international creative city has led to a drastic transformation of the city's social fabric.

While inner-city factories have been rehabilitated and massive urban development has sprawled out to the suburbs, the city of Shanghai further transformed the existing residential areas. In 1990, Shanghai launched a policy of mass demolition and mass reconstruction. In the process, many Shikumen—a distinctive two-to-three story Shanghai-style residential brick housing developed from the late-nineteenth century to the 1920s—were demolished. Over the span of 20 years, the city demolished over 175 million square meters, and over a million households (more than 7.5 million people) were resettled (Zhong & Chen, 2017). Both urbanization and globalization accelerated the transformation of Shanghai's older areas, as both domestic and foreign immigrants gradually replaced the city's original local Shikumen residents (Zhong & Chen, 2017).

In addition, the gentrification of the inner city's formerly industrial sites relegated artists from the city center to the periphery and dispersed them into the suburbs, while allowing other creative industries to cluster in the city. Massive residential complexes in the suburban district of Zhujiajiao, Songjiang, and Anting offered rent-free mixed-usage villas to artists in exchange for a few works of art. Anting New Town, also known as Anting German Town, a Bauhaus-inspired residential complex 30 km on the outskirts of Shanghai, even organized free shuttle buses from downtown to reach the artists' open-studio days. However, with a journey of one hour, the success of the open days and its commercial output was limited.

Nevertheless, the trip offered an almost surreal experience for those who ventured out. Visitors could wander from studio to studio in the gigantesque 50,000-inhabitant capacity ghost town with minimal architecture, parks, and canals, along with few people other than a few gardeners and a lonely convenient store clerk. The real estate developer used the artists as advertising tools, while allowing the artists to take advantage of free rent for a certain period of time. However, by 2015, the city's gentrification process was so developed that those opportunities stopped.

The unstructured bohemian-like effervescence that emerged from Weihai 696 faded out and diluted over the city as artists scattered into different suburbs. A grungy underground space on the north bank of the Huangpu River, at 713 Dong Daming Road, captured best the spirit of these years. DDM Warehouse was a not-for-profit art space financed with the profits of an associated design company. Under the direction of Zheng Weimin (b. 1966), for nine years the space showed an eclectic program. It exhibited local artists, such as the solo shows of Wu Jungyong and Ning Zuohong, as well as group shows like "Useless Life" by Xu Zhen, Yang Zhengzhong, and Yang Fudong. DDM Warehouse also introduced the work of foreign artists like Kristian von Hornsleth and the group Alterazioni Video. Furthermore, it mixed many genres like poetry, ready-made art, and other performative art forms, in addition to hosting punk rock concerts like Torturing Nurse or Brain Failure. It culminated with the participation of DDM Warehouse in the special project section of the 52nd Venice Biennial. The association organized and presented an independently curated exhibition, titled *Migration Addicts* (2007). The show introduced artists with a multiplicity of perspectives from China, Myanmar, the Philippines, Italy, Vietnam, Bangladesh, and the USA. It was an ongoing project two years in the making that investigated how the proliferation of urban spaces redefined social structures. The show questioned how identity was defined in a time of constant migration (ddm warehouse, 2007).

Ironically, the same year DDM Warehouse had to move from its original space, which was under rehabilitation. It settled in Red Town 166, a new creative district at the end of Huaihai West Road. However, DDM Warehouse closed two years later because its shows contrasted with the overall direction of the Red Town management company. The refurbished red brick factory held two museums, the Shanghai Sculpture Space and the Minsheng Art Museum sponsored by the bank of the same name, as well as designers and fashion store retailers like Hong Kong's Joyce Warehouse, cafés, and restaurants. By 2017, Red Town had moved out all tenants and started its second rehabilitation phase. The remodeling was intended to expand the existing site and tear down most of the exhibition buildings. By 2023, the site will host one of the largest commercial hubs in central Shanghai (*Global Times*, 2017).

In the span of a decade, Shanghai gained an image as a cosmopolitan and creative city, partly due to the artists' initial input in the creation of the creative clusters. Weihai 696 marked a further internationalization and cosmopolitanization of the creative industries, with burgeoning and heteroclite forms of art. However, once the transition was accomplished, it appeared more profitable for real estate developers to rent out spaces to the creative industry and other corporations rather than to artists. More specifically, the changing art ecology in Shanghai translated into an entrepreneurial approach that benefited commercial interests. Some artists engaged with hybrid forms, mixing artistic work with commercial work for brands and advertising agencies. As Yin Zhou mentions: "the establishment of MadeIn Company by the conceptual artist Xu Zheng in 2009 was a comment on the necessity of blurred boundaries of production, promotion, support, and curation, especially in the local framework of marketisation within the state-controlled economy" (Zhou, 2015, p. 225).

## 4 The Industry's Institutional Turn

While creative clusters evolved into their commercial form without the presence of artists in all cases, art was still essential for private and state-owned developers. Indeed, in the process of the preparation of the 2010

Shanghai World Expo, the city planned to open 150 museums. The effect of this policy was to transform the institutional landscape of the city. The city demanded that commercial developers provide public amenities and art spaces. Therefore, permissions for real estate development were easier to acquire or were even expedited if spaces for art exhibitions or education were part of the development plan (Zhou, 2015).

Already in the mid-2000s, several privately funded though apparently publicly administrated museums emerged. Most of these were financed by the Shanghai diaspora in Hong Kong or foreign investment. First, the state-owned Duolun Museum opened in 2004. It is considered a state institution even though it is privately run because its museum license was approved at the district level (Zhou, 2015). Then, the MoCa was founded in 2005 by jade tycoon Samuel Kung's foundation, and Zendai was established by former Shanghai real estate mogul Dai Zhikang. They were followed in 2010, at the time of the Shanghai World Expo, by the Minsheng and the Rockbund Museums. The Rockbund Museum is the cultural jewel of the larger redevelopment of the North Bund area, the site of remaining British civic buildings from the Concession Era. The redevelopment was made as a joint venture between the Rockefeller Group and the state-owned Shanghai New Huangpu Group.

While the city's cultural policies aimed at positioning Shanghai as a global creative hub for the World Expo 2010, it was actually after the Expo that the number of museums grew drastically. First, the Power Station of Art was launched in a former electric plant on the site of Expo 2010 as the first state-run contemporary art museum. Since 2012, it has hosted the Shanghai Biennales as well as local and international shows. Following the restructuration of Red Town, Minsheng Art Museum unveiled a new larger site on the right bank of the Huangpu River in 2015: the Shanghai 21st Century Minsheng Art Museum located on the former Expo Pudong site. In 2013, the opening of Shanghai K11 Art Mall by Adrian Cheng, a third-generation Hong Kong tycoon, officialized the marriage of art and commerce. The 278-m tall office and shopping mall offered a dedicated space for exhibition. Situated below the mall at the third basement, the K11 Art Foundation initially showed contemporary art exhibitions and displayed works from its collection between luxury boutiques, staircases, and gourmet restaurants. The concept later opened to modern art. It hosted the first exhibition of Monet in China, called *Master of Impressionism*. Made in collaboration with the Musée Marmottan, the show attracted more than 100,000 visitors, more than the contemporary art exhibition, and forced people to exit through the profitable gift shop.

The year 2017 saw an acceleration of this trend. How Art Museum was founded by Chinese hotelier-collector Zheng Hao. The museum is connected to the Onehome Art Hotel, which also belongs to Zheng. It hosts an impressive permanent collection of Joseph Beuys' artwork and the inaugural show, *Manifesto: Julian Rosefeldt—Works 2005–17*, which takes its name from the German artist's 13-screen video installation. In the installation, actress Cate Blanchett delivers manifestos by more than 50 artists and groups, from the Dadaists to Fluxus. Later the same year, Fosun Group unveiled Fosun Foundation Art Center, which was designed by star architects Thomas Heatherwick and Norman Foster. It was followed by the opening of Powerlong Art Museum from the conglomerate Powerlong Group, which has holdings in real estate, hospitality, battery development, and more; the Center was also backed by a collector and the holding company's founder Xu Jiankang.

2021 saw further add-ons to Shanghai's already considerable collection of museums. Ullens Center for Contemporary Art, originally founded in Beijing by Belgian collectors Guy and Myriam Ullens and now led by the private equity firm Lunar Capital, opened its Shanghai outpost called UCCA Edge. The opening show, *City on the Edge: Art and Shanghai at the Turn of the Millennium*, retraced the rapid social and economic transformation of Shanghai's urban fabric. The exhibition begins with the reproduction of Huang Yong Ping's (1954–2019) *Bank of Sand, Sand of Bank*, a massive sand sculpture representing the 1923 HSBC Shanghai headquarters that slowly disintegrated as time passed. While the work recalls the transformation of Shanghai's economy from its colonial past to its role as a current international financial center, it also mirrors the museum's change of status from a private collector in 2007 to private equity in 2017. Finally, Lujiazui Group, the developing company approved and supported by Shanghai Municipal People's Government, unveiled the Museum of Art Pudong at the heart of Shanghai's financial district of Pudong. The Jean Nouvel-designed waterfront rectangle of marble and glass opened with Cai Guoqiang's firework art retrospective (who already was the first artist of the Rockbund Museum opening), as well as a Joan Miró exhibition; it will further display a collection from the Tate Britain. The Lujiazui Group signed a memorandum of understanding with the institution and aimed to display a national British collection of art from 1500 to the present day.

Downtown Shanghai's transition from a site of art production to a site of art exhibitions is best exemplified in the West Bund project. The West Bund project is an 11 km-long corridor built on the relic of the former Longhua Airport and surrounding site, situated on the north bank of the Huangpu River. Destined to become one of the largest cultural districts in Shanghai, the promenade is part of a larger project that aims to connect the Xuhui District on the waterfront to the historical Bund area. The area covers 9.4 square kilometers and envisages a new cultural district on former industrial land. The area has refurbished and reappropriated former factories and other facilities such as oil tanks and a dome structure that was once Asia's largest cement plant. The area hosts several private museums: Chinese-Indonesian entrepreneur Budi Tek's Yuz Museum and billionaire couple Liu Yiqian and Wang Wei's Long Museum West Bund, established in 2014. It was completed by the private collector Qian Zhibing's Tank in 2019, and to date, the latest institution is a partnership between state-owned enterprise West Bund, the group in charge of the rehabilitation of the area, and French Centre Pompidou. Designed by star architect David Chipperfield, the Centre Pompidou West Bund Museum is "the most significant project for cultural exchange and cooperation between [France and China]," reads Centre Pompidou's press release (2019). All these museums are within walking distance from each other; Tank and West Bund Museums are literally adjacent. Opposite these institutions are the West Bund Art Center, which hosts the West Bund Art & Design Fair, and a few art galleries, including the new Shanghart venue, Aike, and Qian Space. Other galleries have set up in the vicinity, mid-way between West Bund Centre and Yuz Museum, including Dong, Madein, Arario, and Edouard Malingue.

However, the area gives little space for local and emerging artists and focuses on established artists and commercial output. The massive institutions—Yuz is 9,000 square meters, Long has 16,000 square meters of exhibition space and covers an area of 33,000, and Tank project spans over 60,000 square meters—tend to favor famous collections (Monet, Picasso, Pompidou) and artists' retrospectives (Xu Zhen, Ding Yi, Dan Flavin, Olafur Eliasson, Cai Guoqiang, Kaws). Others participate with a commercial group, as when Yuz Museum hosted Gucci's *The Artist Is Present*, curated by Mauricio Cattelan, or the large-scale immersive experience organized by group TeamLab at Tank.

Only two artists have their studios in the West Bund: Ding Yi (b. 1962) and Zhou Tiehai—two artists from M50's golden age. Ding Yi is an internationally recognized artist and qualifies as one of China's most popular and collectable artists (Gaskin, 2015). Since the mid-1980s, he has exclusively created abstract paintings composed of small crosses to create a powerfully intricate ensemble. He received a solo exhibition in 2015 from the Long Museum, a few hundred meters away from his studio. Zhou Tiehai, famous for his critique of the art market with his series of fake magazine covers, developed an agency beyond art productions. Already acting as ShContemporary's art fair local organizer in 2007, Zhou reinvented himself from an artist into a director (Borysevicz, 2007).

Since 2014, Zhou Tiehai officiated as the West Bund Art & Design Fair Director. The fair's first edition was an unusual month-long program, a premier event in the art fair program. Major international galleries, like Gagosian, joined the festival. In the first few days, VIP previews and openings showed the usual crowd of collectors and art connoisseurs; the later days of this format-exhibition fair were intensive for both the participants and visitors. After this initial approach, future fairs returned to the classical three-day format and established collaborations with luxury brands, such as BMW, Dior, and La Prairie.

## 5 Digitalization of the Modes of Production

The growing number of privately owned art museums complements the commercial galleries and the creative hubs in transforming the ecology of art in Shanghai. Although well-established commercial galleries are rejuvenating their panel of artists, many shows include established artists from the older generations. As creative hubs increased rents, artists inexorably moved toward the suburbs. However, they found new ways to create and display their work. Some decided to settle their studio in their home, and a younger generation even migrated toward cyberspace. Artists like Miao Ying (b. 1984) explained that her place of residence is both physical (e.g., Shanghai) and virtual (e.g., the Internet). Works are now often mediated digitally, and many artists work primarily with a computer. In some cases, the computer interface becomes the main tool and subject of the work, like in the 2011 work *Robinson Crusoe* by Lin Ke, a 56-s video loop representing the artist's computer dashboard with wallpaper of a rocky island. The icon of the computer's hard drive, named "Robinson," stands at the bottom of the island. The artists attempted to drag the hard drive icon. The semi-transparent version of the icon moved left and right, as if it was "leaving" the desolated island, before automatically finding its way back to its original place, at the bottom of the rock. Other artists, like Aaaajiao, have even developed virtual environments. In *Space* (2016a), the artist invited audiences to explore a blank web page of ever-changing sizes. Users could scroll up and down, left and right, to a never-ending blank canvas where "websites go to die" (Aaajiao, 2016b). In another work, *Deep Simulator* (2020), a character embodying the user wandered in a virtually generated environment. Aaajiao's digital spaces exemplify new dimensions where artists can create and experiment in the face of the commercialization and financialization of the art ecosystem.

New official media art exhibitions in Shanghai started in the Shanghai Museum during the 2000 Biennale. For its third edition, the exhibition moved away from the traditional forms of Chinese art and crafts (calligraphy, ceramic, ink painting). The organizers appointed the internationally recognized curator Hou Hanru in charge of the project—strategic move that supported the event and built the city's global image (Zhou, 2015). The show embraced foreign artists, like star-artist Matthew Barney, and also marked the first official ventures into new forms of art such as video, installations, and performances (Green & Gardner, 2016). A year later, the China Academy of Art (CAA) in Hangzhou founded the New Media Art Center. In 2003, the Department of New Media was established with courses focused on high-tech and digital media. The department was chaired by Zhang Peili, a pioneer in new media in China and attributed the first video art piece. In 1988, he recorded a video piece, *30 × 30*, in which a piece of glass is repetitively dropped and broken, and then glued back together (Zhou, 2020). CAA was already a ground-breaking institution in the field of video art in 1995 when Qiu Zhijie and Wu Meichun curated *Phenomena/Moving Images: China's Video Art Exhibition*. After the first conference on digital art and the exhibition in Beijing in 2004, Zendai Museum (now renamed Himalayas Museum) hosted *ElectroScape: International New Media Art Exhibition* a year later. The exhibition explored the notion of space and identity in the virtual world and introduced the work of well-known international new media artists. Miltos Manetas exhibited *Super Mario Sleeping* (1997), a humorous take on the video game, where the character falls asleep when the game is not played, or Jin-Jiang Bo's exploration of humans as an interface with *18 Coppermen* (2005), an interactive installation with an acupuncture model.

In 2006, the Shanghai Municipal Committee Publicity Department launched a platform for Electronic Art (Lean, 2007). In 2007, Shanghai

Museum launched Shanghai eARTS Festival (上海电子艺术节 *shanghai dianzi yishu jie*). The Municipal Committee Secretary Wang Zhongwei requested that the festival creates an important new trajectory in cultural development not just by borrowing concepts, but by combining new forms of technological and cultural expression. The festival organizer, under the curation of Victoria Lu, then director of the Shanghai Museum of Contemporary Art, approached several foreign partners, including the Austrian cultural institute Ars Electronica, the German Center for Art and Media ZKM, French Pompidou Centre, Italian communication research center Fabrica, and the US-based university MIT. It was the largest media art festival ever held in China and spread all around the city from the Shanghai Museum of Science and Technology in Pudong to a public display in the Xujiahui CBD. Following the municipality's guideline for combining forms and culture within the festival, CCA professors Xu Qiming and Zhang Peili co-curated the New Media Students' exhibition, where students from the New Media department collaborated with students from Europe and the USA. Zhang Peili described that: "As new media art is a new practice, developing around the world. East and West have common ground and shared opinions" (Zappaterra, 2007). It was the occasion for a younger generation of artists, such as Chen Xiongwei, Aaajiao, and B6, to display their work.

A year later and in preparation for the Shanghai World Expo 2010, where the Expo organizer planned to incorporate the eArts Festival, Shanghai municipality inaugurated the second edition of the eArts Festival. Entitled *Urbanized Landscape*, the ambitious programs aimed at being the largest showcase of digital and new media art in the world. Two curators shared the program, French curator Richard Castelli and Shanghai-based Bizart Davide Quadrio.[1] Like the previous year, international institutions participated in the event. Castelli's *eLandscapes* explored the notion of interactive space. Quadrio, together with Defne Ayas, challenged perceptions of public space with *Final Cut-Processing New Media in Public Space*, a five-day cross-disciplinary performance by musicians, designers, and artists in one of the Xuhui District's busiest shopping and commercial areas. The show featured a participatory journey through virtual images by Feng Mengbo and sound performances by Cheng Xiongwei, Aaajiao, and artist-punk band Top Floor Circus.

[1] http://artasiapacific.com/Magazine/60/BigAmbitionsForNewMediaArtFestivalInShanghai.

Both the 2007 and 2008 eArts festivals were the occasion for mixing digital media and other art forms such as music in performances.

In 2009, however, the festival was much smaller and reduced to three programs due to funding concerns (Li, 2010). The next year, while Shanghai hosted 192 participating countries to celebrate a "Better City, Better Life" for the World Expo, Google services were blocked in Mainland China (Negro, 2017). Facebook was already blocked in 2009. The larger implementation of the Great Firewall, a system of control of the Internet already operational in 2003, coincided with the development of Web 2.0, the introduction of the 4G technology, and the explosion of social media. While the Internet was accessible everywhere with mobile technology, it also became more scattered, controlled, and fragmented, in contrast to Zhang Peili's optimistic view.

Nevertheless, the Great Firewall did not stop artists from experimenting with the digital world in China. It became a source of inspiration for both artists and netizens. They developed a unique mix of emojis, numbers, and a combination of English and Chinese coined as a Martian language. The purpose of this new dialect was to bypass censorship and also influence a specific online aesthetic of low-quality animated GIFs. Within this context, a new generation of artists is particularly prolific. As Ross Holmes (2017) pointed out: "[They] draw attention to the artistic merit and value of mainstream user-generated content, whose visual manifestations frequently range from the banal to the kitsch to the ugly" (p. 22).

While many museums concentrate on established artists, few institutions focus on the younger generation of digital artists. The most influential of these institutions is OCT Contemporary Art Terminal (OCAT), which opened in 2012. The institution is sponsored by Overseas Chinese Town Enterprises, a state-owned amusement park and real estate developer, which was directed by China's digital pioneer Zhang Peili until its closing in 2021. The non-profit art institution focused on media art exhibitions, showcasing major works from the new generation. The second center, Chronus Art Center (CAC), is a smaller non-profit organization, founded in 2013 by entrepreneur Dillion Zhang and situated in M50. CAC developed a system of residency fellowships, lectures, and workshop programs combined with the creation and presentation of media-driven technological art from artists from China and abroad alike. The latest, Shanghai Ming Contemporary Art (McaM), sponsored by Mingyuan Group, yet another property developer, opened in 2015 in the north of Jing'an District. The institution focused on multimedia and performance art. These three institutions distinguished themselves from other museums. They gave a platform for a younger generation of artists, otherwise relegated to their suburban studios and facing the complexities of the commercialization of digital forms.

## 6 Conclusion

Since emerging from the strict frame of Socialist Realism, control of the art industries in China is constantly being negotiated between the state, the market, and the artists. These forces may at times be divergent or aligned; however, they are in general to the disadvantage of artistic freedom. From the city center to the digital world, the same pattern emerges. On the one hand, the market reappropriates the efforts of artists for the benefit of more lucrative creative industries. And on the other, the government's interest in making Shanghai a creative center requires that this be done through evermore institutional constraints, with little to no consideration of young and emerging artists.

After an initial liberalization of the creative forces in the early 1980s, the events of 1989 in Tiananmen Square constrained art to private spaces. The commercialization of art in the mid-1990s gave an initial space for creative experimentation outside the framework of official institutions. Artists were at the forefront of creative industries and helped in popularizing the initial urban creative clusters. However, real estate groups interested in cashing in on their popularity quickly filled creative centers with design companies and other creative industries. Even artists' strategies of self-organization were diminished by their success. The gentrification of downtown creative spaces and refurbished factories inexorably pushed artists further into the city's outskirts.

The continuous development of Shanghai, and the municipal administration's goals in making the city a global creative capital, led to an ever larger scale in infrastructure. The size of investment and private museums revolved around mainstream and established artists. It left few spaces for a younger generation of artists, as there is no state funding for creative entrepreneurs and artists in China (Su, 2008). As a result, artists are scattered in the outskirts of the city and have migrated toward the digital realm. Experimentation within the virtual world is now the norm. However, the art industry is coopting this new frontier for the further financialization of art. The West Bund Group is developing a one-stop art business solution: a complex, mixed large-scale real estate project: the West Bund Media Port, the West Bund AI Valley, and the West Bund Financial Center. It will focus on three core industries: culture and media, technological innovation, and innovative financial industries. The towers are expected to host a new form of creative cluster. It should regroup 20 international galleries, as well as auction house Philips, the Shanghai FTZ International Artwork Exchange Center (SFIAE)—a stock market for the art industry—and AXA Tianping P&C Insurance. The group also signed an agreement with LeFreeport, a bonded warehouse built for the storage of artwork, which was supposed to open in 2017. However, as the industry grows larger, the place for independent artists is more and more at the periphery of Shanghai's art financialization.

## References


Aaajiao. (2016a). *t-h-e-s-p-a-c-e*. Accessed December 1, 2021. https://t-h-e-s-p-a-c-e.com/space/

Aaajiao. (2016b). *t-h-e-s-p-a-c-e*. Accessed December 1, 2021. https://eventstructure.com

Borysevicz, M. (2007, December 20). On Shanghai. *Art Forum*. https://www.artforum.com/print/200710/mathieu-borysevicz-42220

Centre Pompidou. (2019). *Centre Pompidou x West Bund Museum Project Shanghai*. https://www.centrepompidou.fr/en/the-centre-pompidou/international-offers/centre-pompidou-x-west-bund-museum-project-shanghai

ddm warehouse. (2007, April 22). Migration Addicts at La Biennale di Venezia. *E-flux*. https://www.e-flux.com/announcements/40428/migration-addicts-at-la-biennale-di-venezia/

DeBevoise, J. (2014). *Between state and market: Chinese contemporary art in the post-Mao era*. Brill.

Erjavec, A., & Groïs, A. B. (2003). *Postmodernism and the postsocialist condition: Politicized art under late socialism*. University of California Press.

Gao, M. (2003). Post-utopian avant-garde Art in China. In A. Erjavec (Ed.), *Postmodernism and the postsocialist condition, politicized art under late socialism*. University of California Press.

Gao, M. (2012). Changing motivations of Chinese contemporary art since the mid 1990s. *Journal of Visual Art Practice, 11*, 209–219.

Gaskin, S. (2015, July 28). Why is Ding Yi one of China's most popular and collectible artists? *Artnet*. https://news.artnet.com/market/ding-yi-interview-at-long-museum-west-bund-320127

*Global Times*. (2017, July 4). Last days of Red Town. *Global Times*. https://www.globaltimes.cn/page/201707/1054851.shtml

Green, C., & Gardner, A. (2016). *Biennials, triennials, and documenta: The exhibitions that created contemporary art*. Wiley Blackwell.

Gu, X. (2012). The art of re-industrialisation in Shanghai. *Culture Unbound, 4*, 193–221. http://www.cultureunbound.ep.liu.se

Holmes, R. (2017). *Chineternet ugly*. Center for Chinese Contemporary Art.

Lean, W. (2007, October 25). Shanghai eArts Festival. *Art Daily*. https://artdaily.cc/news/22119/Shanghai-eArts-Festival

Li, Z. (2010). 上海私人美术馆调查 (Shanghai private museum report). *LAB Beijing*. https://issuu.com/bjartlab/docs/shanghaipm/11

Negro, G. (2017). *The Internet in China*. Palgrave Macmillan.

Poplin, J. (2017). *Cultural flows in the digital and beyond: The potency of a symbol in Mainland China*. Victoria University.

Rossiter, N. (2006). Creative industries in Beijing: Initial thoughts. *Leonardo, 39*(5), 367–370.

Salmenkari, T. (2004). Implementing and avoiding control: Contemporary art and the Chinese state. *China: An International Journal, 2*, 235–261.

Sheng, Z. (2011). By nature or by nurture: The formation of new economy spaces in Shanghai. *Asian Geographer, 28*(1), 33–49.

Su, N. (2008). *Art factories in Shanghai: Urban regeneration experience of post-industrial district*. National University of Singapore.

Zappaterra, Y. (2007). Digital Fusion. *Design Week, 22*(41), 20–21.

Zhang, X. (2017, October 9). Chinese artist Zhang Xiaogang determined to put Bloodline series to bed. Interview by Enid Tsui. *South China Morning Post*. https://www.scmp.com/culture/arts-entertainment/article/2026094/chinese-artist-zhang-xiaogang-moves-symbolism-surreal

Zhong, X., & Chen, X. (2017). Demolition, rehabilitation, and conservation: Heritage in Shanghai's urban regeneration, 1990–2015. *Journal of Architecture and Urbanism, 41*(2), 82–91.

Zhou, Y. (2015). *Growing ecologies of contemporary art: Vignettes from Shanghai*. University of California Press.

Zhou, Y. (2020). *A history of contemporary Chinese Art, 1949 to present*. Springer.

CHAPTER 4

# Addictive Technologies? The Moral and Normative Dynamics Shaping the Chinese Gaming Culture

*Thomas Amadieu*

## 1 Introduction

The Chinese video game industry has become a major economic player, capable of producing and publishing blockbusters for the huge domestic market and international export. China has the largest number of online gamers in the world—518 million as of December 2020 (China Internet Network Information Center [CNNIC], 2021). It has also two of the largest global game corporations by revenue, Tencent and Netease. In

This chapter has been presented and benefitted from comments at the 13th Congress of the European Sociological Association.

T. Amadieu (✉)
ESSCA School of Management, Paris, France
e-mail: thomas.amadieu@essca.fr



S. Chrétien-Ichikawa and K. Pawlik (eds.), *Creative Industries and Digital Transformation in China*,
https://doi.org/10.1007/978-981-19-3049-2_4

2021, China's domestic gaming revenues rose more than 6.4% to 296.5 billion yuan (US$46.6 billion) (Game Publishing Committee of the China Audio-Video and Digital Publishing Association, 2021). Video games have also become an institutionalized form of competition called eSport and a form of entertainment to watch on streaming platforms. *League of Legend* or *Dota 2* tournaments attract huge audiences, both online and in arenas. Shanghai presents itself as the capital of eSport, and in an effort to compete, the Beijing authorities have launched the "E-sports Beijing 2020" initiative that aims to "provide major subsidies to teams, arenas and video games that promote local culture" (Ye, 2021a). Thanks to this institutional recognition, video games are an integral part of Chinese consumer culture and are now an international projection of soft power.

This spectacular expansion has not been without hitches and resistance. The history of gaming in China is tumultuous: Chinese psychiatry was the first to recognize video gaming as a potentially addictive disorder and its use was illegal for a long time, as games were perceived as a harmful foreign influence for youth, giving rise to episodes that some scholars have labeled as "moral panic" (Cao & Downing, 2008; Golub & Lingley, 2008; Szablewicz, 2010). Thus, in 2018, the release of new video games was temporarily suspended in order to redefine the authorization criteria in terms of content; in 2019, a curfew on online games was imposed for minors. In 2021, a much discussed maximum of three hours per week of online gaming for minors was decided. The international press has widely echoed these measures, often seeing them as a sign of a new "cultural revolution" or, at the very least, a restriction of freedoms seemingly inconceivable elsewhere.

Video games are in fact at the heart of normative tensions linked to the inherent characteristics of the activity itself but also to the complex relations maintained by China with cultural practices. At the same time, video games are a source of technological influence and the promoter of an imaginary "branded tradition." In addition, they are a source of problems for young people in terms of mental health ("addiction"), physical development (myopia, sloth, weight gain, sleep quality), and academic success. This ambivalence is also that of the State, which oscillates between policies encouraging eSports and the development of a powerful gaming industry on the one hand, and crackdowns on Internet cafés (*wangba*) and drastic supervision measures on the other. Gaming is valued as a symbol of China's growing influence and the influence of its techno-culture, while also viewed as a "spiritual opium" that stigmatizes their violence and harmful influences.

In China, as elsewhere in the world, the platform economy, including gaming devices, is at the heart of different types of moral tensions. Should the content be censored because of its potentially harmful consequences on users (in terms of violence, pornography, representations of the world and values conveyed)? Should the national market be protected from foreign productions? Should access be limited for certain categories of the population? What types of regulations should be put in place to limit the effects of Internet or gaming addiction? As Balsiger & Schiller-Merkens (2019) pointed out, answering these questions involves asking what is right or wrong, just or unjust, legitimate or illegitimate. This leads to debates and struggles between actors with competing interests and values.

As a cultural practice, video games are endowed with an uncertain legitimacy (Styhre et al., 2018). The academic world is no stranger to this issue, as one of the major tropes of the field of Game Studies is to legitimize games, whether from the point of view of narrative richness (Tavinor, 2009), the continuity with "noble" forms of play because of the cognitive or motor skills involved (Besombes & Maillot, 2020), or the positive impact on well-being (Barr & Copeland-Stewart, 2021).[1] Demonstrating its educational virtues, or at the very least demonstrating the player's agency (Muriel & Crawford, 2020) and creativity, appears crucial.

It is around the issue of addiction that tensions crystallize. Addiction to online gaming was recognized early on in China as a form of behavioral disorder in its own right and is a massive and central social phenomenon. Beyond the tragic events reported in the press, several surveys have revealed high levels of addiction in China compared to other countries: the prevalence of Internet Gaming Disorder (IGD) among adolescents has been estimated as high as 17% (Liao et al., 2020). The condition "may result in negative outcomes such as depression, anxiety, academic dysfunction, poor sleep quality, exacerbating relationships with family and peers, and even substance use" (Liao et al., 2020).

[1] A scientific journal such as *Games and Cultures* illustrates such a perspective.

Due to technological innovations and the development of a unique business model, the Chinese gaming industry is based more than elsewhere on a logic of "gamblification," i.e., the introduction of gambling features involving random rewards in exchange for real money (Brock & Johnson, 2021). China is a pioneer in the exploitation of the "freemium" games model—with Shanda in 2005—a model based not on the purchase of products (video games), but on the payment of virtual objects included in the games and often indispensable to win ("pay-to-win"). This profound transformation of video game design has not been sufficiently explored to understand the dynamics of addiction (Zendle & Cairns, 2018). In this chapter, I explore how the moral dimensions but also the registers of justification (notably scientific) contribute to shape a singular ludic culture and an original governmentalization of players.

## 2 A Comprehensive Perspective on Gaming in China

In China, most of the studies on video games focus on policies or adopt a business studies perspective. Few studies focus on the cultural aspects of the practice. The latter ignore the issue of addiction, which is viewed with skepticism or ignored altogether. Yet it is impossible to understand the development of this cultural industry and the upheavals that characterize it without integrating this crucial dimension. The development of a video game culture impregnated with gambling is at the heart of current political and moral tensions. Of course, China is not the only country facing the transformation of the social meaning of games and their uses, but it is more prevalent in China due to the early development of the "free-to-play" smartphone game model.

The sociological and cultural studies on digital culture in China that have multiplied in recent years tend to adopt a constructivist approach: addiction is seen as the result of episodes of moral panic (Szablewicz, 2010), assigning a stigmatizing label to practices that appear threatening to parents, teachers, and authorities in general (Bax, 2016; Manjikian, 2016). Game Studies, in general, are marked, more or less explicitly or consciously, by a desire to rehabilitate and valorize the practice, since the cultural legitimacy of the practice seems to them to be insufficient in comparison with other forms of cultural production. The focus on Internet or gaming addiction is consequently perceived as necessarily the result of power struggle and paternalistic ideology.

In her book, Szablewicz (2020), for example, proposed an anthropological approach to trace the "narratives" surrounding digital gaming and to draw up a "topography" of it. The author's analysis of the Internet café is that of a refuge, a space of freedom where young people can escape the particularly high expectations placed by society on individuals. The pressure of the public and then of the authorities led to medicalization via the creation of a new clinical disorder; this development follows a classic constructivist pattern: Internet and gaming addiction is essentially associated by Szablewicz (2020) with a discourse and a "rhetorical construction rife with inconsistency" (p. 102).

The Chinese field lends itself particularly well to the constructivist approach, due to the strongly political coloring of cultural practices in China. The arts and the media are major political issues, so everything related to the framing of practice can be read through the Foucauldian prism of bio-power or authoritarian governmentality of the youth. In this light, the regulations of the video game market and its consumption are seen as extensions of the State's hold on the interstices of freedom offered by video games. The way Internet cafes (*wang ba*) have been controlled and closed down is interpreted as a political will of social control, as well as a response to parents' fears of unruly, unproductive youth and unhealthy lifestyles. In this perspective, moral and political concerns related to gaming and digital uses tend to be assimilated to irrational or even dangerous attitudes, such as moral panics (a state of panic generally characterized by frightened crowds that leads to erratic behavior).

However, a growing number of studies are making it possible to grasp what is at stake in the most extreme forms of gaming practice in the context of rapid technological and commercial evolution. In particular, the gamblification of video games is gaining growing attention (Brock & Johnson, 2021). The irruption of these game designs into the world of video games profoundly modifies their uses, creating new hybridizations between game worlds. It invites us to renew discussions on the manner in which the game industries shape our digital uses and can be the source of genuine social and health problems. The rapid and profound evolution of the social meanings of video games "forces" the decoupling of Game Studies and the question of addictions generated by certain game devices.

Adopting a stance of axiological neutrality is crucial in the face of an object that is strongly marked morally, for which ideologically opposed positions clash, and offers a source of axiological tensions, including among the population of gamers themselves.

## 3 A Powerful Gaming Industry Shaped by the State

From the outset, the emergence of the video game industry in China was marked by a context of normative tension, mainly around the effects they produce on the youth. Several historical studies have emphasized that the arrival of video games, initially as imported products, was initially perceived as a danger. Video games represented a source of corruption of youth in the face of Western hedonism and consumerism, as well as a distraction from studies, work, or other social activities (Zhang, 2012). Video games immediately aroused a distrust that is still evident today in the use of the expression "spiritual opium" in a major Chinese journal in the summer 2021 (Chong, 2021). Thus, strict supervision or prohibition prevailed for many years, and game consoles in particular were banned for more than a decade.

The contents of video games, like all forms of cultural production, are subject to censorship by the authorities so that they are in line with the values promoted by the Party. As stipulated in Article 3 of the Regulations on Publication Administration of State Council of P. R. China, culture "shall persist in the direction of serving the people and socialism" (State Council of P. R. China, 2011). These forms of censorship have intensified recently, with new guidelines prohibiting games that produce "blurred moral boundaries," that promote a revisionist form of history, or appeared more culturally Japanese than Chinese (Ye, 2021b). Recognizing the cultural importance of video games, regulatory authorities reaffirm their moral importance: "games are a new art form that must highlight 'correct values'" (Ye, 2021c). Among the latest developments, it is worth mentioning the desire to eliminate "effeminate" portrayal of men in games.

However, the gaming craze has not been curbed even with intense regulation, especially with the success of Internet cafés, which have made up for the originally low level of PC equipment in the general population. For a long time, the State was in a reactive logic: letting market forces operate, then taking radical measures to regain control ("crackdown") when confronted with a crime or event attracting popular attention. For example, 130,000 Internet cafés were dismantled in the years following the murder of 25 young people in a fire in 2002, and rules requiring the reduction of virtual rewards for gamers in cafés beyond three hours of play were imposed, even though they were easily circumvented (Dyer-Witheford & De Peuter, 2009).

But the State exhibits a complex relationship with video games, beyond the attitude of defiance toward a practice that would be considered uniformly harmful, which is described above. Video games on PCs have also been perceived as an educational and modernization opportunity, a form of leisure allowing the development of digital capital and skills. Thus, as Zhang (2012) pointed out, "video-gaming technologies were instrumental in educating young people about modern technologies and Western culture-knowledge essential to improving the general quality [...] of China's labor force" (p. 2397). In post-socialist China, a dialectic of discourses around video games as an imported technological innovation, which veered between pathology and productivity, emerged starting in the 1980s. According to Zhang (2012), the contradictory discourses around video games reveal the contradictions of values among individuals and a Chinese society where the deep economic transformations and the economic opening to globalization have not been accompanied by political changes. As Zhang (2012) stated, "socialist tradition and rising neoliberalism make odd bedfellows" (p. 2394). In fact, different social actors are struggling for power and cultural legitimacy in the context of the State's strengthening control over commercial activity and citizens' behavior.

The relationship between the State and video games is not just a neat dichotomy; the two are in fact intertwined in many ways, which explains the ambivalence of the relationship and the inherent tensions. The State has played an active role in the rise of the gaming industry. This has been done on two main levels: *protectionism* toward the tech giants and the recognition of *eSport* as a form of sport in its own right.

The video game industry has been shaped by the State and its various institutions. The objective, inspired by the Korean example, has been to foster a powerful but controlled private sector, helping Chinese companies to dominate the domestic market. The strategy was carried out in three stages: import, substitution, and creation (Liu, 2013). As a sign of success, the creativity of the gaming industry is now recognized, with considerable success stories (see for instance the game *Genshin Impact*). These conditions of emergence have been shaped by both the ministries competing for their regulation and the commercial interests of gaming companies. As Ernkvist and Ström (2008) pointed out, although the industry has been remarkably innovative, the "online game industry in

China was deeply enmeshed in and shaped by three national policy objectives: a) techno-nationalism, b) information control and c) social fears, and pragmatic nationalism" (p. 121). In principle, video games as cultural products should fit into the Party's agenda, as a tool of propaganda and soft power (Chung & Fung, 2013). Despite this, the creativity of games produced in China is undeniable. The creativity is not only visible in the narratives or in the gameplays, but it is also manifested in marketing and design.

A second aspect that has contributed to the rise of video games is the institutional recognition by assimilating it into the field of sports. Several milestones mark the will to legitimize the practice. As early as 2003, China recognized eSport as an official sport. The Ministry of Education made it an undergraduate major and the profession was officially recognized. These recognition efforts have contributed to the creation of a complete ecosystem, with regular official competitions (*League of Legends* championships for example, see Fig. 1), the organization of events and competitions, match broadcasting devices, commentary programs, etc. As Yu (2018) pointed out,

> live eSports competitions are presented as media spectacles that nurture the ideal patriotic citizen, just like any other major events-for instance, the Olympics or the national games; accordingly, eSports has become a platform to display carefully crafted nationalism and China's soft power. (p. 93)

## 4 The Problematic Uses of Gaming in China: A Nation of Gamers?

The official recognition and economic importance of gaming do not prevent debates in China, particularly scientific ones, about the effects on health of casual as well as professional gaming. Thus, in an article written by several Chinese researchers from the Shanghai University of Sport (Yin et al., 2020) published in the *Journal of Sport Health Science*, the researchers questioned the benefits/costs of gaming for the well-being and health of eSport athletes and practitioners in general. If eSport has beneficial aspects, similar to other sports ("motor skills, mental agility, processing speed, executive function, motivation, and, to a lesser extent, physical exertion [...] building skills related to cognitive ability,

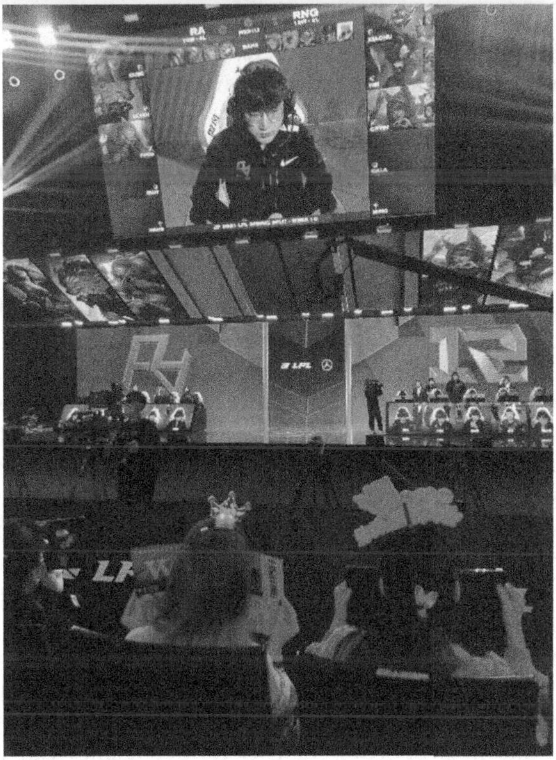


**Fig. 1** Fans supporting their eSport champions during a live event in Shanghai in 2021 (*Source* Picture taken by the author during the LOL competition in Shanghai, June 2021)

reading ability, reaction time, and sensorimotor skills"), numerous costs are associated with eSport activity:

> The intensity of training required for competitive eSports games paradoxically necessitates sitting in the same position for hours at a time in front of a computer or television screen, enduring high levels of stress, visual attention, blue light (from light-emitting diodes), and repetitive small-muscle movements, which together equate to a sedentary and, consequently, unhealthy lifestyle. (Yin et al., 2020, p. 486)

Authors also include other negative outcomes such as "stress, sleep disturbances, vision problems, musculoskeletal pain, overuse injuries, metabolic disorders or weight gain, and other behavioral problems (i.e., addiction, violence, aggression)" (Yin et al., 2020, p. 486). Besides eSport athletes, often very young, appear to be "suffering from precarity, and facing disposable futures" (Lin & Zhao, 2020, p. 595).

Beyond eSports, gaming in China seems to be considerably more intense than elsewhere in the world and raises a number of issues. According to a recent survey conducted in 2020 and 2021 among gamers over 18 years old in several countries, "Chinese gamers played an average of 12.4 hours per week, exceeding the U.S. average of 7.7 hours per week and the global average of 8.5 hours per week" (Limelight Network, 2021). Among them, 17.6% spend more than 20 hours per week on the activity, compared to 6.2% in Germany for example, or 9% in South Korea.

In the survey, we also learn that gamers watch an average of 3.3 hours per week of other people playing online (on streaming platforms) and 3.9 hours of eSport tournaments (e.g., *League of Legends* championships). This is more time spent than watching traditional sports. Chinese survey respondent also reported more often that their daily activities have been altered by gaming, with 39% having missed a shower, 39.8% a meal, and 38.2% sleep due to playing a video game. The use of video games in the workplace is also unique in China, with 71.2% of working gamers playing video games at work, including 34.6% who say they play every day.

For a significant proportion of users, video games can lead to loss of control and harmful consequences on their health. The most recent update of the American Psychiatric Association's Diagnostic and Statistical Manual of Mental Disorders includes Internet gaming disorder as a condition warranting further study, and the revision of the International Statistical Classification of Diseases (ICD-11) by the World Health Organization (2018) mentioned gaming disorder under the category "Disorders due to substance use or addictive behaviours."

A meta-analysis published in 2018 (Long et al., 2018) based on 36 relevant studies published in Chinese (involving 362,328 participants in total) revealed that "the prevalence rates of POG in China range from 3.5 to 17%, which is higher than those reported worldwide" (p. 359). It suggests that vocational school students and unemployed youth are more vulnerable. The high prevalence of problem gaming can be explained by various factors, with several studies mentioning the strong pressure exerted on young people by Chinese society (Bax, 2014), the considerable popularity of eSports, or even the diagnostic tools used (Stevens et al., 2020). Another avenue that has not been widely explored in the literature is the structure of the gaming on offer in China, which differs from other regions of the world (notably Europe and the United States), consisting primarily of smartphone games available "24/7" and including micro-transaction devices that are reputedly more addictive (Zendle & Cairns, 2018).

The scientific results of these studies have political effects since they justify measures to control and regulate gaming practices. In this respect, China can rely on an abundant scientific literature, produced by Chinese researchers who themselves have an influence on the recognition of the disorder by the WHO and international health authorities. For instance, Dr. Wei Hao was a member of a work group on development of diagnostic guidance of ICD-11 on substance use-related disorders, and he participated in or organized WHO expert meetings on gaming disorders. Along with a panel of experts, he is the author of a notice in 2019 (for the English version see Xiang et al., 2019) formulating a set of findings on the context entitled "Expert Consensus on the Prevention and Treatment of Gaming Disorder in China" (2019 edition).

Gaming was medicalized early in China, with recognition by Chinese psychiatry as early as the early 2000s, in contrast to doubts previously raised by American psychiatry about the nature of the disorder. The contrast with the relative indifference to gambling addiction may be due to the need to channel criticism of a popular activity. Indeed, the expansion of industries producing negative externalities on its users contributes to the pathologization of overconsumption, as the medical discourse focuses attention on the individual problems of a minority of gamblers or gamers losing control (Amadieu, 2021).

## 5 Addictions by Design: The Gamblification of Video Gaming

Why is there such a prevalence of intense levels of gaming practice? This is partly the result of the regulation of gaming in China and the specific forms taken by the market. First, the prohibition of home consoles (from 2000 to 2015), which are still the most popular type of gaming in the United States, Japan, and Europe, has led to a shift to mobile phones. Local developers have invested in the smartphone gaming market more than anywhere else in the world. By promoting and protecting national champions whose core business is social networks (Tencent) and Internet search engines (Alibaba), the government has helped shape a smartphone-driven gaming industry. But the particularity of online games is that they are easy to access and often free of charge, thus attracting a very large audience. As an example, *Honor of King*, an immensely popular game in China, was developed for smartphones by Tencent, with a connection to WeChat to reinforce the community aspect. The mini-games in WeChat are intended to socialize the largest audience (1 billion users) to the game, attracting novice, often elderly, players. At the same time, the encouragement of digital use, especially for surveillance and monitoring of the pandemic, contributes to the widespread use of smartphones.

Furthermore, the business model of Internet platforms is mainly based on maximizing engagement. As a result, the logic of "pay-to-play" and "loot boxes" was imposed early in China. That is, games that are designed to promote spending behaviors, often with use of "dark patterns," are prohibited.

As pointed out by Chew (2019), these new local behemoths have not Sinicized the game market, contrary to the official narrative. Local adaptations and creations have always been prominent. The early commercial success of Shanda (listed on NSADAQ in 2004) was mostly due to more advanced marketing policies, such as winning over new users in medium-sized cities. China has observed the explosion of developers and publishers. In a capitalist logic of accumulation and concentration, the sector is now dominated by several large groups. The consequence is that video games have become the core of the profitability of tech companies that have acquired their place as world leaders through various acquisitions. The logic of profitability drives a process of commodification of this type of cultural production, which has deleterious consequences on creativity (Chew, 2019).

At the heart of the development model that shapes contemporary video game design and uses is a central phenomenon: gamblification. The monetization mechanics based on the use of real money for the exchange of in-game virtual objects was not invented in China, but very early on these elements took a central place here. This is due to several factors: the first one is the appearance of gold farms, Chinese gamers professionalizing themselves in virtual production in order to make money. In their analysis of these forms of prosumers, several articles have pointed out that in the globalized ecosystem of video games, some Chinese players understood very early how to make money from games (Heeks, 2008).

Another factor is the early adoption of a business model dominated by developers, which can be described as a "virtual item and service retailer" model (Chew, 2019, p. 204): games are free, but some virtual products are paid for. In 2006, for the first time the game Zhengtu Online (ZTO) offered an extremely popular game mechanic based entirely on the search for treasures, with gambling-like features. These mechanics are inspired by the *kompu gacha*, gambling-like game mechanics found in Japanese games. Very quickly this gameplay model became the norm in China. This business model generates huge profits and is imitated by the Western gaming industry. These types of gaming structures have become ubiquitous, whether on Steam or Apple Store platforms, in Great Britain or in China.

Gamblification is detrimental to the creativity of game designers and has even become a source of contempt among gaming communities ("Chinese style online games," called *guochanyouxi*). The logic of game design is deeply changed. It is now based on monetization through the adoption of lottery-type devices, which allow the player to acquire a chance to win items valued in the game (characters, skins, weapons, etc.). The game evolves from being a cultural "product" to a "service," which is consumed for a defined time and/or segment. In addition to "loot boxes," there is "skins gambling" (i.e., gambling on, inter alia, eSports tournament results using in-game cosmetic items, including those obtained from loot boxes). This hybridization process has been identified as a form of gamblification of video games: the mechanics of random rewards play an increasingly central part in the game.

Studies are accumulating that underline their danger in terms of addiction (Drummond et al., 2020). The real cost of these expenditures is often ignored by gamers; especially in the long term, addiction leads to a loss of control over consumption. Despite this, loot boxes are omnipresent in mobile games, which dominate the market in China. Compared to other markets, loot boxes are much more present and have become almost the norm, as shown in a recent article that reviewed the 100 most popular video games in China in an impressive review (Xiao et al., 2021): 91 games include loot boxes, and of games deemed suitable for children aged 12+, 90.5% contained loot boxes. Authors have explained that this is significantly higher than the 59% found by a recent and comparable UK study (Zendle et al., 2020) and the 62% found by an Australian study (Rockloff et al., 2020).

However, this type of system leads to an extremely unbalanced distribution of expenses: a minority of players, the "whales" in gambling jargon, represent the majority of revenues from the gambling industry. A study conducted in China demonstrated that "the majority of loot box revenue is generated by the top 10% of spenders: indeed, the top 1% alone generated 26.3% of all revenue" (Zendle et al., 2020, p. 2). These high spenders are most often negatively impacted by these expenditures, especially if they are very young and vulnerable audiences (Fig. 2). But their high profitability makes them desirable to companies.

In short, the particular configuration of the Chinese gaming industry explains in part the various problems encountered by a large fraction of Chinese youth. The domination of online gaming on smartphones, coupled with the import of gambling mechanics at the heart of gameplay, forms a combination conducive to problematic uses. By banning home consoles and encouraging national platforms to dominate the market, a more harmful form of video games has come to be more prevalent.

## 6 Governmentalization of Youth Gaming

Faced with this reality, the regulation of gaming in China is based on a justification that is intended to be scientific. It relies on two main elements: the regulation of loot boxes and the control of uses.

### *Regulation of Loot Boxes*

China has been a pioneer in regulating the practice of loot boxes by requiring the industry to disclose the probabilities of obtaining randomized rewards from loot boxes as early as 2017. This is a very liberal choice, based on the idea of a rational and informed consumer. Moreover, the Entertainment Software Association, the American union of video game companies, has proposed in 2019 as a self-regulation the obligation to reveal the probabilities of loot boxes "to help consumers make informed choices about their purchases" (ESA, 2019). Apple has required loot box probability disclosures for all games available on the iOS platform worldwide since December 2017 but does not actively enforce this requirement (Xiao, 2020b). So, this approach is favored by the industry in different countries in their self-regulation. Would the PRC's approach be consistent with that of the market when it is self-regulating? This soft approach, informing the consumer, is favored in other areas in the West, and one

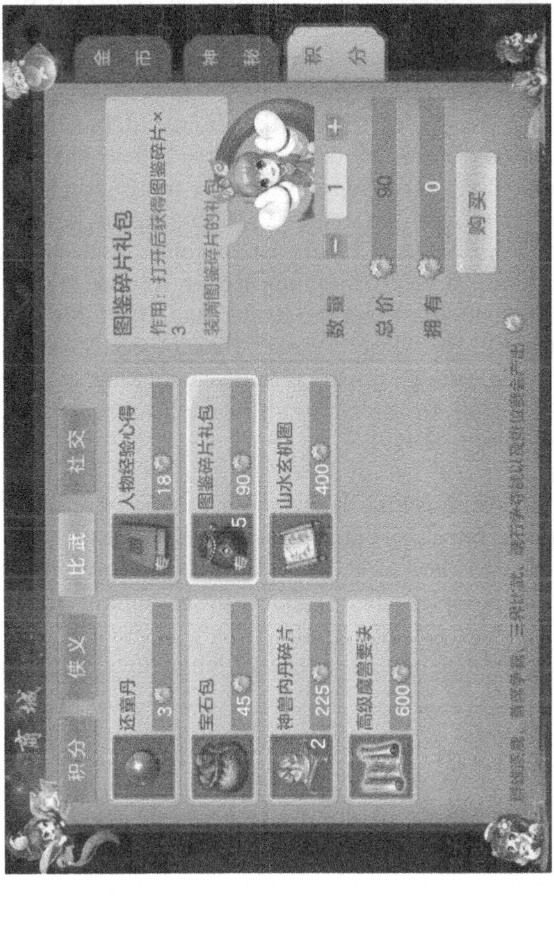


**Fig. 2** Loot Boxes in a Chinese Game (*Source* Screenshot from dataset produced by Xiao et al. [2021])

article compares it to nudge (Newall et al., 2020), but companies can seek to reduce the effectiveness of nudge (complicate the message, hide it, etc.). The addictive industries (tobacco, alcohol, gambling) have long practiced "sludge" or "dark nudges," circumventing the legal obligations to inform consumers.

In fact, what appears from a survey (Xiao et al., 2021) is that most probability disclosures were made suboptimally; that is, information on the probability of winning is very difficult to identify or understand. Companies are implementing responsible gambling policies, such as pity-timers, which allow the player to win the desired item after a given number of transactions. However, some experts believe that these are sludges, as they can increase the illusion that the more money one bets, the more likely one is to win. These self-regulating approaches can therefore reinforce cognitive biases. Chinese law requires disclosure if these devices are used. Limits are certainly imposed on minors regarding the amounts of in-game spending (Xiao & Henderson, 2019). But these caps are considered too high by some experts, while others (funded by the industry) consider the setting of caps as ineffective (King & Delfabbro, 2019). They do not apply to adults (South Korea had imposed and then abandoned the measure in 2019).

The paradox is therefore that on the crucial issue of gamblification, the regulation is rather soft and liberal. How can this be explained? Could it be because the industry's profitability depends on it? China, which prohibits gambling, does not seem to place these measures at the heart of its response. For example, when defining the minimum age required to play a game, it is above all the content of the games (e.g., violence, gore, sexuality) rather than the existence of transactions that enter into consideration.

### *Regulation of Behaviors*

The regulation of the gaming industry has always focused primarily on the youth population, particularly juveniles. A review of the proposed rationale for the latest legislation is instructive. Starting from September 2021, minors are allowed to play online games only between 8 p.m. and 9 p.m. on Fridays, Saturdays, Sundays, and public holidays (Goh, 2021). The simplicity of the measure and its highly coercive nature has attracted considerable attention worldwide to what is seen as potentially the most restrictive regulation in the world. Nevertheless, it requires several remarks. Firstly, it follows similar measures taken in recent years to reduce the amount of time spent by minors on video games, so it is not a complete novelty. Moreover, it only concerns children under 18 years old and only online games; other types of games on consoles (admittedly less used in China) or on PC (offline) are not concerned because of the impossibility of implementing it.

An examination of articles related to this law published in the official press, in particular *Xinhua*, *People's Daily*, and *China Daily*, sheds light on the importance of scientific justification for the measure: the American Psychiatric Association is cited as a reference, as well as studies by researchers from Rutgers University, the WHO and research data from China, and a professor from the prestigious Tsinghua University in Beijing (Wu, 2021).

The rationale for targeting adolescents is based primarily on the concept of addiction: "They are prone to overuse online games and even become addicted," mentions the National Press and Publication Administration to Xinhua News Agency, and "Protecting their physical and mental health is vital" (Li, 2021). According to the administration, other activities better suited to education and health should be promoted: "Allowing less time for online games will help guide minors to physical exercise and social activities that are better for study and health" (Li, 2021). Offline games are presented as healthier, probably because they do not have the same consequences in terms of addiction: "The notice is aimed only at online games. As for healthy offline ones, parents and their children can decide the time themselves," mentions the article from *China Daily* (Li, 2021). And on the justification for leaving an hour despite all, the regulator highlights the health benefits of certain games: "We leave one hour for minors to play online games because some teachers and parents said that they understand and accept minors' moderate exposure to the games, especially healthy ones including sports games, programming and chess" (Li, 2021).

The scientific underpinning of the measure is widely underlined, as it is at the core of the justification regime. But a moral coloration is not absent either. The official press articulates a medical and scientific type of rationality with considerations related to morality. This is particularly evident in the insistence on imposing not only a constraint on uses, but also in the grammar of making children, parents, and teachers responsible. To make the consumer feel responsible and guilty is a strategy also adopted in other forms of addictive consumptions, be it processed foods or gambling. In contrast to the scientific studies on addiction that draw attention to the risks of stigmatizing people who lose control, the need to control oneself and to educate people to be passionate about the real world is emphasized in state-media: "young children should learn to control themselves and properly manage their time"/ "They [parents and teachers] should suggest more healthy and productive activities that can cultivate the youths' passion for real life—in the real world" (Zhao, 2021).

The measures are also embedded in the more ideological framework of a renewal of the nation, as evidenced by the declaration of the Press and Publications Administration. The declaration alludes to a campaign by Chinese President Xi Jinping to cultivate a healthier society for a more powerful China: "Adolescents are the future of the motherland and protecting the physical and mental health of minors is related to the vital interests of masses, and in cultivating newcomers in the era of national rejuvenation" (Goh, 2021).

The preoccupation with moral values is also put forward, especially concerning the control of contents. For the governmental news agency Xinhua, the control of video game content must also include "removing obscene and violent content and avoid money-worship and effeminacy" (Xinhua, 2021).

In response to these measures, the industry was asked to emphasize its social responsibility and to implement control measures. In a form of scene setting, the local authorities of Shanghai and the Communist Party's central propaganda department in Beijing have summoned the main actors of the sector to call them to responsibility: "Companies must elevate their political standing and deeply recognise the importance and urgency of preventing minors from becoming addicted to online games." They added that "games with a "wrong set of values," including money worship and "gay love," need to be bypassed" (Ye, 2021c).

In an effort to comply with these injunctions, Tencent has set up Midnight Patrol, which consists of mobilizing facial recognition technologies to control that the youngest do not play beyond the limit set. This goes beyond the law to demonstrate the company's responsibility. The company has also set up a broader system allowing parents to control the digital gaming behavior of their children, including "tools to track and limit the playing time and spending habits of minors" (Tencent, 2021). Systems like the "Parental Guardian Platform" and "Healthy Gameplay

System" are designed to inform parents and allow them to monitor remotely their child gaming habits (Hollister, 2021).

The grammar of responsibility is adopted to accommodate Chinese characteristics. It involves digital control through apps for parents and teachers, in a kind of techno-control at the service of the State. This is very different from the West and from liberal market economies, where controversial industries react to consumers and citizens' concerns by putting in place largely "cosmetic" responsibility tools, as in the case of gambling. In China, in a context of state capitalism, it is above all a matter of complying with state injunctions.

Nevertheless, the effectiveness of consumer governmental measures in reducing addiction is debated. Xiao (2020) pointed out that the law is only for minors; it does not offer a solution for young adults. Curfew measures on games are not always effective as we can see from the example of South Korea, which imposed restrictions on minors' access to video games as early as 2011. According to Choi et al. (2018), the measure did not have the expected effectiveness. No lasting effect was observed on the number of hours spent on the Internet by young people and on Internet addition. Even if identity control can be better enforced now, thanks to facial recognition, there are many ways to circumvent these devices and the regulation is not always applied with much diligence. Among the techniques mentioned by players are borrowing the account of parents or grandparents (with their consent or without their knowledge) and renting the accounts of adults or using a VPN to play abroad. The creativity of young Chinese Internet users seems to be infinite in this respect.

## 7 Conclusion

Gaming has become an integral and important aspect of Chinese culture. The gaming industry now occupies a central place in the broader ecosystem of creative industries, with new hybridizations between gaming and the entertainment industry, the eSport spectacle becoming dominant on platforms and leading to the professionalization of e-athletes. As in other fields, China has managed in a few years to move from an imitation model to original creations. The arrival of online games with network technologies and the active support of the State have contributed to foster a powerful Chinese gaming industry. Its economic weight, as well as all the ways to capitalize on games (different professions in the sector), has contributed to make China a nation of gamers. Today, creations like

*Genshin Impact* are successfully exported around the world and praised for the Chinese coloration it gives to the global gaming culture. But also decried by many players because of its logic based on mechanisms similar to gambling. This last example is enlightening about the contradictions and tensions surrounding the Chinese video game culture and its place in the world.

For, even if gaming as a leisure activity has become mainstream, it is not entirely trivialized. The uses of the Internet and video games have raised many legitimate questions since their beginnings, around the problem of overuse and its consequences on vulnerable populations and its cost for society. In the same way that social media are now at the heart of moral concerns about their effects of manipulation, addiction, and harms (Bhargava & Velasquez, 2021), video games are also the object of moral concerns. China stands out for its own response to a problem that affects the world at large. The country combines market dynamics driven by technological innovation and protectionism, but also uses a form of digital marketing creativity that is fundamentally ethically problematic.

Video games are a window of observation on the developments of Chinese "platform capitalism" and the attempts to define its specific forms (with Chinese characteristics) with its own value systems, integrated into global value chains. At the heart of these hybridizations of this platform economy, increasingly under fire for the effects they produce on our societies and our sanity, China has developed its own ecosystem, with a particular type of governmentality that echoes the "authoritarian liberalism" coined by Keane (2013). By seeking to shape a thriving national video game industry, the Chinese authorities have also contributed to the development of certain social problems that they seek to control through surveillance and control of contents and users. There is no doubt that the observed and constantly shifting evolutions of the video game market will have an influence.

The issue of moralizing markets and capitalism is not unique to China. Companies, especially if they are accused of producing externalities, are pursuing corporate social responsibility (CSR) policies and are now defining their societal or environmental mission. The question of legitimization runs through the studies on controversial industries. While some industries have long sought to "moralize" their practices, particularly with regard to addiction, the video game industry has been relatively inactive until the last few years. The upheaval induced by the gamblification of video games may change this.

Gamblification remains a blind spot in studies of the game industry and game culture in China. The addictive dimension of these devices that are colonizing the world of video games leads to a major modification of the uses and meaning of the practice. Rapid hybridizations threaten the growing legitimacy of video games over the last decades. Could it be that the positive narrative about the 9th art or eSport and its educational, sporting, or narrative virtues are partly annihilated by the irruption of gamblification mechanisms?

## References

Amadieu, T. (2021). *La fabrique de l'addiction aux jeux d'argent* [The making of gambling addiction]. Le Bord de L'eau.

Balsiger, P., & Schiller-Merkens, S. (Eds.). (2019). Moral struggles in and around markets. In *The contested moralities of markets*. Emerald Publishing Limited.

Barr, M., & Copeland-Stewart, A. (2021). Playing video games during the COVID-19 pandemic and effects on players' well-being. *Games and Culture, 17*. https://doi.org/10.1177/15554120211017036

Bax, T. (2014). Internet addiction in China: The battle for the hearts and minds of youth. *Deviant Behavior, 35*(9), 687–702.

Bax, T. (2016). "Internet gaming disorder" in China: Biomedical sickness or sociological badness? *Games and Culture, 11*(3), 233–255.

Besombes, N., & Maillot, P. (2020). Body involvement in video gaming as a support for physical and cognitive learning. *Games and Culture, 15*(5), 565–584.

Bhargava, V. R., & Velasquez, M. (2021). Ethics of the attention economy: The problem of social media addiction. *Business Ethics Quarterly, 31*(3), 321–359.

Brock, T., & Johnson, M. (2021). The gamblification of digital games. *Journal of Consumer Culture, 21*(1), 3–13.

Cao, Y., & Downing, J. D. H. (2008). The realities of virtual play: Video games and their industry in China. *Media, Culture & Society, 30*(4), 515–529.

Chew, M. M. (2019). A critical cultural history of online games in China, 1995–2015. *Games and Culture, 14*(3), 195–215.

China Internet Network Information Center (CNNIC). (2021). *The 47th Statistical Report on China's Internet Development*. https://www.cnnic.com.cn/IDR/ReportDownloads/202104/P020210420557302172744.pdf

Choi, J., Cho, H., Lee, S., Kim, J., & Park, E. C. (2018). Effect of the online game shutdown policy on internet use, internet addiction, and sleeping hours in Korean adolescents. *Journal of Adolescent Health, 62*(5), 548–555.

Chong, K. P. (2021). Tencent sinks after China denounces online gaming. *The Wall Street Journal*.https://www.wsj.com/articles/tencent-plummets-as-china-takes-aim-at-online-videogames-11627962018

Chung, P., & Fung, A. (2013). Internet development and the commercialization of online gaming in China. In N. B. Huntemann & B. Aslinger (Eds.), *Gaming globally: Critical media studies* (pp. 233–250). Palgrave Macmillan.

Drummond, A., Sauer, J. D., Hall, L. C., Zendle, D., & Loudon, M. R. (2020). Why loot boxes could be regulated as gambling. *Nature Human Behaviour, 4*(10), 986–988.

Dyer-Witheford, N., & De Peuter, G. (2009). *Games of empire: Global capitalism and video games*. University of Minnesota Press.

Ernkvist, M., & Ström, P. (2008). Enmeshed in games with the government: Governmental policies and the development of the Chinese online game industry. *Journal of Games and Culture, 3*(1), 98–126.

ESA. (2019). *Video Game Industry Commitments to Further Inform Consumer Purchases*. https://www.theesa.com/news/video-game-industry-commitments-to-further-inform-consumer-purchases/

Goh, B. (2021). Three hours a week: Play time's over for China's young video gamers. *Reuters*. https://www.reuters.com/world/china/china-rolls-out-new-rules-minors-online-gaming-xinhua-2021-08-30/

Golub, A., & Lingley, K. (2008). "Just like the Qing Empire": Internet addiction, MMOGs, and moral crisis in contemporary China. *Games and Culture, 3*(1), 59–75.

Heeks, R. (2008). *Current analysis and future research agenda on 'gold farming': Real-world production in developing countries for the virtual economies of online games* (Development Informatics Working Paper No. 32).

Hollister, S. (2021). How Tencent's sweeping new facial scans will catch Chinese kids playing past curfew. *The Verge*. https://www.theverge.com/2021/7/9/22567029/tencent-china-facial-recognition-honor-of-kings-game-for-peace

Keane, M. (2013). *Creative industries in China: Art, design, and media*. Wiley.

King, D. L., & Delfabbro, P. H. (2019). Video game monetization (eg, 'loot boxes'): A blueprint for practical social responsibility measures. *International Journal of Mental Health and Addiction, 17*(1), 166–179.

Li, H. (2021). Stricter limits on minors' online gaming. *China Daily*. https://www.chinadaily.com.cn/a/202108/30/WS612cc4a0a310efa1bd66c215.html

Liao, Z., Huang, Q ., Huang, S., Tan, L., Shao, T., Fang, T., Chen, X., Lin, S., Qi, J., Cai, Y., & Shen, H. (2020). Prevalence of Internet Gaming Disorder and its association with personality traits and gaming characteristics among Chinese adolescent gamers. *Frontiers in Psychiatry, 11*, 1266.

Limelight Networks. (2021). *Market research the state of online gaming*.

Liu, C. (2013). Raising the golden Lin, Z., & Zhao, Y. (2020). Self-enterprising eSports: Meritocracy, precarity, and disposability of eSports players in China. *International Journal of Cultural Studies, 23*(4), 582–599.

Long, J., Liu, T., Liu, Y., Hao, W., Maurage, P., & Billieux, J. (2018). Prevalence and correlates of problematic online gaming: A systematic review of the evidence published in Chinese. *Current Addiction Reports, 5*(3), 359–371.

Macey, J., & Hamari, J. (2019). eSports, skins and loot boxes: Participants, practices and problematic behaviour associated with emergent forms of gambling. *New Media & Society, 21*(1), 20–41.

Manjikian, M. (2016). *Threat talk: The comparative politics of Internet addiction*. Routledge.

Muriel, D., & Crawford, G. (2020). Video games and agency in contemporary society. *Games and Culture, 15*(2), 138–157.

Newall, P., Walasek, L., Ludvig, E., & Rockloff, M. (2020). Nudge versus sludge in gambling warning labels, *PsyArXiv Preprints*.

Rockloff, M., Russell, A. M., Greer, N. M., Lolé, L., Hing, N., & Browne, M. (2020). *Loot boxes: Are they grooming youth for gambling*. NSW Responsible Gambling Fund.

State Council of P. R. China [国务院] (2011): 出版管理条例 [The Regulations on Publication Administration]. Visited on 30 June 2022, http://english.www.gov.cn/archive/laws_regulations/.

Stevens, M. W., Dorstyn, D., Delfabbro, P. H., & King, D. L. (2020). Global prevalence of gaming disorder: A systematic review and meta-analysis. *Australian & New Zealand Journal of Psychiatry, 55*(6). https://doi.org/10.1177/0004867420962851.

Styhre, A., Szczepanska, A. M., & Remneland-Wikhamn, B. (2018). Consecrating video games as cultural artifacts: Intellectual legitimation as a source of industry renewal. *Scandinavian Journal of Management, 34*(1), 22–28.

Szablewicz, M. (2010). The ill effects of "opium for the spirit": A critical cultural analysis of China's Internet addiction moral panic. *Chinese Journal of Communication, 3*(4), 453–470.

Szablewicz, M. (2020). *Mapping digital game culture in China: From Internet addicts to eSports athletes*. Springer Nature.

Tavinor, G. (2009). *The art of videogames*. Wiley.

Tencent. (2021). 哪个小朋友还没下线? https://mp.weixin.qq.com/s/Cr17TKWQ3XcuNzDw085OLw

Wu, C. (2021). GAME OVER: China imposes world's strictest limits on video games. *People's Daily Online*. http://en.people.cn/n3/2021/0913/c90000-9895444.html

Xiang, Y. T., Jin, Y., Zhang, L., Li, L., Ungvari, G. S., Ng, C. H., Zhao, M., & Hao, W. (2020). An overview of the expert consensus on the prevention and treatment of gaming disorder in China (2019 Edition). *Neuroscience Bulletin, 36*(7), 825–828.

Xiao, L. Y. (2020b). Conceptualising the loot box transaction as a gamble between the purchasing player and the video game company. *International Journal of Mental Health and Addiction*, 1–3.

Xiao, L. Y., & Henderson, L. L. (2019). Towards an ethical game design solution to loot boxes: a commentary on King and Delfabbro. *International Journal of Mental Health and Addiction, 19*(1), 177–192.

Xiao, L. Y., Henderson, L. L., Yang, Y., & Newall, P. W. (2021). Gaming the system: suboptimal compliance with loot box probability disclosure regulations in China. *Behavioural Public Policy*, 1–27.

Xinhua. (2021). *Chinese authorities summon online game platforms for talks.* http://www.news.cn/english/2021-09/09/c_1310176131.htm

Ye, J. (2021a). Chinese Communist Party aims to turn Beijing into an e-sports hub, backed by subsidy schemes. *South China Morning Post*. https://www.scmp.com/tech/policy/article/3097701/chinese-communist-party-aims-turn-beijing-e-sports-hub-backed-subsidy?module=inline&pgtype=article

Ye, J. (2021b). New video game approvals dry up in China as internal memo shows that developers now have many red lines to avoid. *South China Morning Post*.https://www.scmp.com/tech/policy/article/3150622/new-game-approvals-dry-china-internal-memo-shows-developers-now-have

Ye, J. (2021c). Shanghai summons video gaming companies for a lecture as city follows up on government drive to protect minors. *South China Morning Post*. https://www.scmp.com/tech/big-tech/article/3148723/shanghai-summons-video-gaming-companies-lecture-city-follows

Yin, K., Zi, Y., Zhuang, W., Gao, Y., Tong, Y., Song, L., & Liu, Y. (2020). Linking Esports to health risks and benefits: Current knowledge and future research needs. *Journal of Sport and Health Science, 9*(6), 485.

Yu, H. (2018). Game on: The rise of the esports middle Kingdom. *Media Industries Journal, 5*(1), 89–98.

Zendle, D., & Cairns, P. (2018). Video game loot boxes are linked to problem gambling: Results of a large-scale survey. *PLoS ONE, 13*(11), e0206767.

Zendle, D., Petrovskaya, E., & Wardle, H. (2020). *How do loot boxes make money? An analysis of a very large dataset of real Chinese CSGO loot box openings*. https://doi.org/10.31234/osf.io/5k2sy

Zhang, X. (2012). Censorship and digital games localisation in China. *Meta, 57*(2), 338–350.

Zhao, M. (2021). As with all things, moderation is key in gaming: To the point, *China Daily*. https://www.chinadaily.com.cn/a/202108/31/WS612d9e18a310efa1bd66c531.html

CHAPTER 5

# Mediatization in Fashion: A Focus on the Rise of Reflective Emotions Within China's Digital Ecosystem

*Gabriele Goretti*

## 1 Background: The Digital Landscape in China

The impact of China's digital landscape has emerged globally with terrific strength, becoming a significant epicenter of innovation and investments. To understand the reasons for this impressive success, we have to look back to the steps that characterized this process.

In 1978, China took major steps to open up and develop the economy, which was accompanied by a concerted effort to raise the level of science and technology in the country (Piek, 2008; Tidrick, 1986; Xiaojuan, 1997). A major turning point in the history of technology in China was 1992, when liberalization, reform, and foreign investment were heavily promoted in the Southern provinces. The Chinese government's policy

G. Goretti (✉)
Jiangnan University, Wuxi, China
e-mail: gabriele.goretti@qq.com





S. Chrétien-Ichikawa and K. Pawlik (eds.), *Creative Industries and Digital Transformation in China*,
https://doi.org/10.1007/978-981-19-3049-2_5

toward foreign investment shifted dramatically, offering, for the first time, significant domestic market access to firms that brought in advanced technology. The government provided more market access to foreign investors, among which were many multinational corporations (Fig. 1).

Accession to the WTO in 2001 is one of the last big contributing factors in China's process of technological advancement and ushered in a new phase. In the process of accession, China committed to eliminating various regulatory measures which imposed restrictions on foreign technology transfer. Newly emerging industries benefitted from this arrangement, including telecommunications, banking, insurance, professional services, and commercial distribution, all of which were flooded with foreign investment.

As a result of the government's long-term strategy to pilot more technology originating in China, during the course of 2013, the number of active smart devices grew from 380 to 700 million. The Chinese e-commerce market emerged as a global leader. In fact, on Singles Day, online marketplaces like Taobao and Tmall posted more than RMB 36 billion (almost $6 billion) in sales in just 24 hours. Users make some five billion daily searches (China Mobile Internet, 2013, Overview) through Baidu, and hundreds of millions communicate via WeChat, Tencent's mobile messaging app. Now with 632 million users—and counting—the

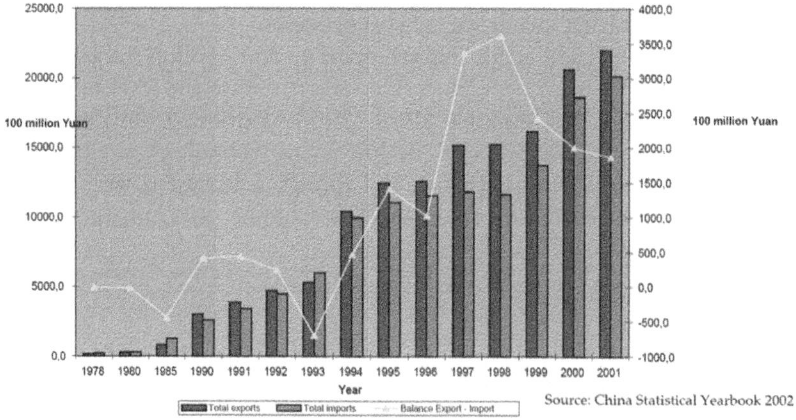


**Fig. 1** Value of imports and exports in China (*Source* China Statistical Yearbook 2002)

Internet is fundamentally altering the fabric of daily life in China (China Internet Network Information Center, 2014) (Fig. 2).

In 2019 the Internet Information Center (CNNIC) released the 43rd "Statistical Report on the Development of China's Internet Network," which shows that until December 2018, the number of Internet users in China was 829 million, with a total of 56.53 million new internet users and the Internet penetration rate reached 59.6%, an increase of 3.8% from the end of 2017. At that time, the number of mobile Internet users in China reached 871 million, and the number of mobile Internet users increased by 64.33 million. The proportion of Internet users with mobile phones increased from 97.5% at the end of 2017 to 98.6% at the end of 2018. From the statistics, we know that mobile Internet access has become one of the most common channels for Internet users, and that China has entered the digital economy (Jingting, 2019).

Chinese e-commerce was almost non-existent 10 years ago. Now it is a major sales channel for retailers, with combined sales of about RMB 1.3 trillion (US$211 billion) in 2012, second only to the USA. In 2014 it was the largest e-commerce channel in the world. This is partial because China's fast-tracking IT industry has been one of the key elements in

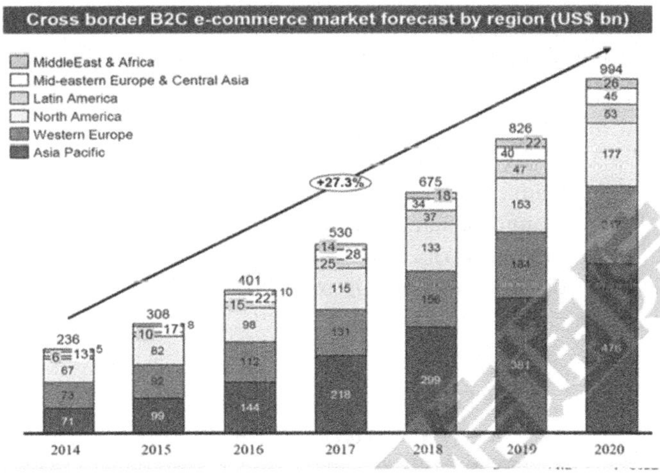


**Fig. 2** Market global B2C cross-border e-commerce during 2016–2020 (*Source* Aliresearch)

China's 10th Five-Year Plan, with an emphasis on making digital television and broadband affordable and available. Now with more than 10 million broadband subscribers, 70 million Internet users, 200 million plus mobile phone subscribers, and potentially many millions of digital television users, China is a huge market for digital content.

Within this context, China reformed its cultural sector through informatization (*xinxihua*), a term widely used in China to describe the uptake of information and communication technology (ICT). The development of the Internet, digital technologies, and social media removes the economic barriers to knowledge-sharing and the exchange of ideas (Lessig, 2008, p. 83) Cost-saving technology and peer-to-peer cyberspace offer participants easier involvement and interplay with free expression (Williams, 2014, p. 47). In this new setting, expanding digital participation and increasing media awareness became part of a positive lifestyle and "a democratic way of sharing information" (Park, 2014, p. 72).

Winston Ma (2017) describes the digital landscape of China's mobile economy and the influence of China's Big Three "BAT" (Baidu, Alibaba, and Tencent). He explains the characteristics of the e-commerce boom in China: "Chinese customers are migrating to the mobile internet rapidly. Because China has the largest smartphone user population in the world, the trend of 'going mobile' has taken off with greater speed than anywhere else in the world" (p. 7).

The promotion and popularization of ICT in China can act as an effective intervention for the preservation, continuity, spread, and recreation of cultural industries. According to Keane (2004), since the end of the 1990s China developed a "cultural technology transfer" that takes into account the dynamics of flows of information and creativity, whereby measurable economic benefit accrues to the appropriator, often at the expense of the originator of content. However, the spread of ICT allows opportunities for more individuals to benefit from participating in the cultural ecosystem.

## 2 Enthusiasm for Technology Among Chinese Netizens

In China, young people are mainstream consumers in the digital marketplace, representing 35% of the total number of customers in 2020. They are attracted to new products and technologies, have strong brand loyalty, and are dependent on smartphones. In addition, they are usually very optimistic about their future earnings and development. These users are usually called young "netizens," keen users of the Internet for whom digital entertainment is not just for leisure time, but also part of their social life; they share their gaming and other experiences with enthusiasm on the net, thereby creating a type of digital community (China Entertainment and Media Outlook, 2016–2020, PWC).

Chinese netizens' user experiences present two main characteristics. First of all, they look for information through passive engagement with information targeted to them through movies or video. The second characteristic is their affinity with social media, in which the fans have a substantial impact on the production and distribution of content. Kantar Social Media's 2016 report indicates that one-third of social media users in China are from the post-1990s generation, which has led many brands to adapt their communication and sales strategies based on this segment and social media trends.

Moreover, it should be noted that young Chinese consumers place more trust in the information they get on the Internet than what they receive through traditional channels of communication, such as television and print media. This trust in online sources has led to a wide dissemination and use of QR codes, particularly codes printed in newspapers, magazines, and billboards that allow individuals to directly access an online page via smartphone.

A significant example of the affinity of the Chinese netizen to social networks is represented in the rise of Internet celebrities. From 2014 to 2015, the number of fans of Internet celebrities exploded from 100 to 310 million people, leading brands to reshape their marketing campaigns. By investing in celebrity spokespeople, brands intend to develop their users' awareness and improve their market share. In 2016, the industrial output value generated through the influence of internet celebrities has been evaluated at 58 billion yuan (Zhang, 2019).

The pervasive effect of young Chinese netizens' use of apps and other functions of smartphones have transformed Chinese citizens' lifestyles. Apps with distinct functions have become integral to the daily life of Chinese youth and changed the lifestyle of netizens, largely due to their portability. According to the results of the 43rd "Statistical Report on the Development of China's Internet Network" (2019), we know that before December 2018 the number of apps in the Chinese market had reached 4,490,000. The top three areas are games, life services, and e-commerce. There are 1,380,000 game apps (30.7%), 542,000 life service apps (12.1%), and 421,000 e-commerce apps (9.4%).

## 3 Emotions and the Chinese Digital Ecosystem

Digital emotions can be defined as human emotions that are primarily influenced, augmented, composed, or expressed through digital technology. This technology can be a direct digital interface we control, such as a smartphone or kiosk screen, or data collected from sensors embedded in objects or environments around us that are used to affect our experience in that moment (Avery Dennison Report, 2017). Whereas physical emotions are expressed simultaneously through individual voice and body language, digital emotions are experienced through contextual content, experiences, and services that can be stored, edited, and analytically interrogated at vast scale in the digital sphere. Consequently, digital emotions have the potential to open a new window into our understanding of the human experience in a "connected world" (Lotto, 2017, p. 11).

According to recent literature, digital emotions are more contagious than physical emotions, thus they present a more pervasive effect (Kramer et al., 2014) owing to the speed of dialogue and the virality of digital communications. Online communities are bigger and broader, so messages travel farther and faster across generations, time, space, and cultures than they do in the purely physical world. New media are developing systems and languages to indicate and communicate Digital Emotion (Derks et al., 2008; Walther, 1992) and their existence demonstrates that people experience and express their emotions online in different ways.

Zhang Jingting (2019) pays special attention to the situation of the sharing economy in China by relating the consumption and the sensibilities of the Chinese in Society 4.0. Based on the analysis of the concept of *tianxia* in Chinese philosophy,[1] Jingting (2019) believes that the rapid development of the sharing economy in China may offer the space for sharing emotions.

[1] The classical idea of *tianxia* has become the focus of debate in scholarship and public discourse. Literally meaning "all under heaven," *tianxia* refers to a system of governance held together by a regime of culture and values that transcend racial and geographical boundaries (more on this later) (Wang, 2017).

Jingrong Tong (2015) states that, in the public space, to the Internet makes it possible for individuals to express their emotions, as well as to share collective sentiments. In this sphere, emotions are important factors for knowing about and manifesting public life. Cyberspace offers the public space to show their interests and feelings about issues that affect the society (Figs. 3 and 4).

When talking about emotions and consumption among Chinese netizens, Lihui Geng and Xiaoli Li (2018) try to find the emotional relationship between consumption and brand loyalty. According to Geng and Li's (2018) use of attributional theory, there are three attributional dimensions of emotions: the locus of causality, controllability, and the stability of emotions. They believe that there is a potential area in which the causes of emotions may affect consumers' post-purchase behaviors. Product attributes and marketing communication may cause the consumer to experience emotions as well. Moreover, Jahyun Song and Hailin Qu (2018) investigated how focus is related to customers' value perceptions. They realized that not every perceived hedonic value leads to satisfaction

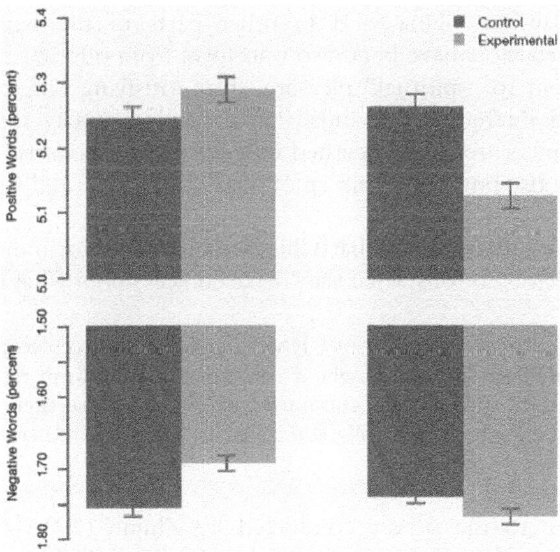


**Fig. 3** China's netizens' massive-scale emotional contagion (*Source* Kramer et al. [2014])

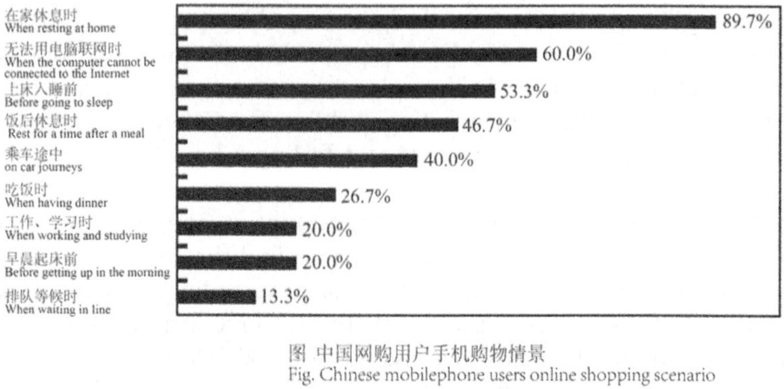


**Fig. 4** The moment of consumption of Chinese netizens (*Source* Liu & Song, 2018)

unless the product generates positive emotions in the customers (Song & Qu, 2018).

According to the perspective offered by Song and Qu, we can notice that nowadays in China, and in other parts of the world as well, consumer behaviors have begun to transform from offering simple material enjoyment to "spiritual" pleasure, from satisfying tangible demands to satisfying intangible demands. Thus, consumers pay for their feelings. Customers are not concerned only about the quantity, quality, and price of goods, but also their emotional satisfaction and psychological engagement.

Li Zhijun (2016) states that Chinese consumers are more and more driven by their emotions when they make choices about what to consume:

> The multi-year precipitation of China's rapid economic development has enabled domestic urban household consumers to transform rapidly from "price seekers" to emotional consumers, which means that their consumption views have been gradually controlled by emotions rather than more rational choices. (p. 100)

According to the survey conducted by Zhijun (2016), the author believes that at least half of middle-class families will become the new mainstream consumers, which is a major shift occurring now. In addition, Chinese consumers are becoming emotionally more unpredictable:

"In the era of emotional consumption, emotions can create wealth and create brands. The value of emotional consumption is limitless" (p. 101). In order to carry out emotionally targeted marketing, enterprises must abandon the price war, because price-based marketing cannot match the trend of emotional consumption, and it is also bad for the long-term development of enterprises.

## 4 Digital Emotional Levels and Fashion: Focus on Chinese Netizen Users

Media and the related interactive processes put the "screen" of the digital product at the center of the user experience (UX). Desmet and Hekkert (2007) define product experience as "the entire set of affects that is elicited by the interaction between a user and a product. The emotional experience, as the feelings emotions that are elicited, is part of this complex cluster of affects" (p. 60).

Donald Norman (2005) proposes that the emotional system consists of three different, yet interconnected levels, each of which influences our experience of the world. The three levels are visceral, behavioral, and reflective. The visceral level is responsible for the ingrained, automatic, and almost animalistic qualities of human emotion, which are mostly out of our control. The behavioral level refers to the controlled aspects of human action, where we unconsciously analyze a situation so as to develop goal-directed strategies. The reflective level is, as Donald Norman (2005) states that the home of reflection, conscious learning on new concepts and generalizations on relevant concepts.

Recent research reports offer that Chinese users spend at least six hours per day on their phone. Yet, the average attention of a Chinese consumer on their phone is 1.7 seconds, compared to 2.5 seconds on a computer and 8 seconds of physical attention (fashionchinaagency.com, 2021). With the increasing amount of content created and shared on a daily basis, the audience is then looking for an additional richness: immediate, sensational, experiential, and emotionally unique.

For consumers motivated by hedonic values, the experience itself is important (Babin et al., 1994). These consumers enjoy the experience without the need to make a purchase, but a purchase may be the result of the experience. Hedonic values can include a desire for entertainment and escapism or enjoyment of the hunt for a good bargain (Babin et al., 1994). Hedonic values also positively influence consumers' attitudes toward social network advertising (Anderson et al., 2014).

Today, the most desired brands aim at developing playful interactive experiences, taking inspiration from what surrounds the users and communicating content that is easy to watch and remember. By "playful interaction" we refer to an activity in which the user's effort is rewarded with a pleasant improvement of skills (Goretti et al., 2020). The process is also characterized by the presence of stimulated emotions through and thanks to the use of the device. It is possible to distinguish three different levels of playful interaction: selection, activation, and guidance. The first level is related to the user interface enrichment by game mechanics that aim only for pleasure. Playful activation replaces basic interactions with small challenges that aim to increase the attention and interest of the user. Finally, playful guidance provides integrated, just-in-time learning, help, and hints as satisfying rewards or achievements. Brands need to constantly reinvent themselves in a more premium and unique way (fashionchinaagency.com, 2021) in order to keep creating playful interactions. It is essential to catch and retain the customer's attention by considering media concentration (TV, print, outdoor, and radio), as well as media fragmentation (360° communication connection touchpoints).

Users evolve in a constant quest for new and innovative content, including videos and different kinds of graphics. We can distinguish three kinds of experiences among Chinese netizens that characterize the UX: on-the-go, lean forward, and lean back. "*On-the-go*" scenarios represent 70% of fashion communication market (Jingting, 2019), as Chinese people are used to watching content on public transport or while walking. Adapted content like GIFs, short videos, Weibo topics, or vertical formats are created and continuously updated. Content must be impactful in order to stay in consumers' minds with such a short attention span.

In addition to "on-the-go" consumption of media, there are other potential digital interactions. The "*lean forward*" model represents 20% of the market (Jingting, 2019). Within lean-forward moments, digital content is consumed during waiting moments and longer transport rides. Chinese customers have become accustomed to passing the time with entertaining or interesting content. In this model, content like WeChat mini-programs[2] represents an effective way to catch the consumer's attention. In these contexts, the brand shares something with its audience and the user enjoys spending quality time on specific subjects and values.

There are also emerging "*lean back*" user scenarios (10% of the market), which include a longer period of time in the user's digital journey (Jingting, 2019). For example, articles of two pages or more or mini-programs on WeChat focus on significant aspects of offered products or services. This is a unique time to create a more meaningful connection with the audience, thanks to long posts, videos, or live-streaming sessions.

Even if fast and playful communication experiences cover the majority of the digital communication market, we can highlight the potential for brands to engage in conversations and create new and intense relations with Chinese users (especially among young customers). For example, Chinese Millennials are more sensitive than older generations to issues such as sustainability or gender equity. They value brands' commitment to wider engagement. Luxury activism is rising as an emerging topic in digital interaction by "not only share what you stand for but what you fight for" (fashionchinaagency.com, 2021). For instance, Yves Saint Laurent Beauty launched a worldwide campaign called "Abuse Is Not Loved" to raise awareness of domestic abuse. Such a significant social commitment is a new key value in making young customers identify with the brands. Then, considering the emerging commitments of Chinese netizens in supporting values and emerging challenges, we can highlight the rise of a new space for intellectual content in digital experiences; products and brands act not only as status symbols but as icons of values and socially positive behaviors.

Below we compare digitalization in both the Western and Chinese contexts by focusing our lens on the world of fashion in particular.

[2] WeChat mini-programs are "sub-applications" within the WeChat ecosystem. They enable to provide advanced features to users such as e-commerce, virtual store tour, task management, coupons, and other services.

## 5 The Mediatization of Fashion in the West and China

### *Mediatization Processes in the Western Fashion System*

To understand the role of digitalization in Chinese fashion, it helps to relate what happened in the Western fashion system as a point of comparison. Consequently, we have to highlight how China uniquely implemented and evolved digital applications developed abroad.

Many designers and researchers point to the role of social media in changing practices at all levels of the fashion industry. The designer Albert Elbaz, Art Director of the French fashion brand Lanvin, hints at the possible transformations of fashion practices related to the proliferation of social media. Elbaz explains the significance of these changes by applying the notion of *mediatization*, presenting various practices in fashion that has become shaped by and for digital media (Rocamora, 2016). He describes mediatization as "the production of fashion, such as the staging of catwalk shows and the design of collections, being molded by and for the media, transforming retail practices and everyday consumption" (p. 1). In fact, the media have become increasingly central to shaping practices and experiences in fashion. Since the early 2000s some consistent innovations and strengths in the Western fashion system, in particular in relation to fashion shows, include the use of digital short films, fashion blogs, and social media interactions.

The Western market represents the cradle of the cluster of players that generated the traditional fashion system and its media operators. Thus, fashion shows—as presentations of new collections and as outputs of a complex supply chain—have always been accompanied by a media system. Fashion magazines—in close synergy with photographic images, cinema, television and, in recent decades, websites and social networking platforms—have contributed, in parallel with the fashion show, to disseminating stylistic innovations to the public.

For years now, the fashion system has defined communication in the digital sphere as one of the most effective ways for consumers to interact with brands, thus overcoming the traditional mediator role played by the traditional fashion media and journalists. The expansion of electronic media into the fashion show environment has manifested itself, not only in terms of the presence of media devices and digital users in the usual performance stages, but also in the transformation of social interactions around fashion week.

In 2008, when fashion brands started experimenting with digital short films, they were implemented and diffused via websites. As a medium, digital film offers innovators a new artistic outlet; it also allows brands to communicate their visions directly to an online audience of millions, outside the institutional fashion circuit, and without the production, travel, and indeed environmental costs of a traditional fashion show. The fashion show has become a more "totalized" performance, communicated and diffused through virtual networks (Menkes, 2010).

In 2010 a small number of designers such as Hussein Chalayan and Yves Saint Laurent embraced screen fashion films for their seasonal fashion shows, presenting them directly at global fashion weeks. However, attendees expecting a live performance were largely unimpressed with a film shown in lieu of a live fashion show. Even though many fashion insiders presented concerns about the introduction of these presentation tools, fashion film has stood as a distinct conceptual and/or commercial medium in fashion (Uhlirova, 2013). However, fashion film has not generally become a substitute for the fashion show in terms of its industrial or aesthetic functions; instead, the fashion show has become "mediated" by screen-based user experiences, which often present the focal emotional concept of fashion collections at fashion weeks.

Another piece of the digitalization of the fashion world is the evolution of blogs and social media since their initial appearance in 2001 (Rocamora, 2016). Blogs have created a platform for individuals with a recreational or professional interest in fashion to submit commentaries or post photographs of their own sartorial choices or those of others, allowing more people to participate this new interactive stage of fashion. Scholars consider 2009 to be the year in which personal fashion bloggers and street style bloggers attained visible influence in the industry. Since that time, bloggers are regular invitees to fashion shows, often sitting in the first and second rows of fashion shows (Findlay, 2015). For example, at the Spring/Summer 2010 show in Milan, Dolce & Gabbana invited bloggers Garance Doré, Scott Schuman, Tommy Ton, and Bryan Grey Yambao (Bryanboy) to attend.

Another important effect of top-down support for digitalization is the rise of social media in fashion. Social networks today permeate every aspect of our lives and provide us with the tools to relate to others, extend our productivity, and nurture our interests. Mobile devices, wireless networks, and apps allow us to produce content in real time and to take advantage of online services, facilitating the direct connection between people, technologies, and brands (Prunesti, 2016).

Social media is now part of every marketing decision an organization takes. To succeed and to emerge from the huge variety of products advertised, a company must be present everywhere. The important thing is not to be deeply present in some social media but, rather, to be everywhere at once to expose the consumer to the constant influence of the brand's image and the product itself (Pan, 2019). Consumers' tastes and preferences in terms of social media advertisements are shifting too, from emotional content that tends to resonate more with users to entertaining and fun ads. Therefore, it is important that luxury fashion brands always keep up-to-date with evolving tendencies (Pan, 2019).

### *China's Rise in Fashion Mediatization*

According to McKinsey's China Luxury Report 2017 (McKinsey Institute, 2017), the luxury market in China reached €537 million in 2016, representing 32% of the total value of the sector. This percentage almost tripled compared to the weight of China in the sector in 2008 and is expected to reach 44% in 2025 (McKinsey Institute, 2017). According to this perspective, China's luxury fashion market in 2021 is boosted by 1.5 million consumers who each spend more than 40,000 yuan ($6,255) per year on fashion-related luxury products. As a group, they are responsible for 81% of the sector's total sales over the past 12 months, according to a new research report from consulting firm Oliver Wyman Report (2021) (Fig. 5).

To understand how the use of digital devices has grown so much and why they are so significant in China's fashion market, we have to relate to significant programs implemented within the last 10 years, since China's 12th Five-Year Program outlined a strategy to integrate creativity and technology innovation in 2011. This long-term strategy leads to a parallel evolution between creative industries and digital tools and platforms, which moreover attracts foreign investors interested in this ecosystem. A macro-effect of this strategy is the strong rise of e-commerce platforms in fashion and other creative sectors.

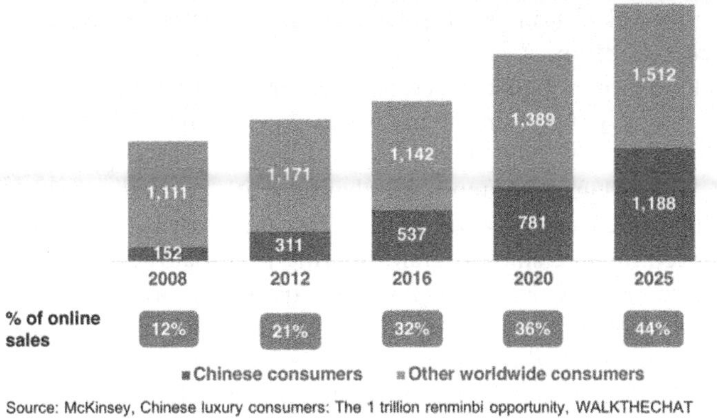


**Fig. 5** China luxury market and worldwide one (*Source* McKinsey)

Thus, since 2015, China has become the largest e-commerce market in the world, with an estimated $630 billion in sales, according to McKinsey's report in 2016. Despite the recent global financial crisis and the consequent sluggish growth in international trade, China's cross-border e-commerce has maintained a growth rate of about 30%. In fact, from 2008 to 2015, its turnover grew from CNY 800 billion (around $123 billion) to CNY 5.2 trillion (around $0.8 trillion). China's cross-border e-commerce imports and exports reached 1.69 trillion yuan (about 260.9 billion U.S. dollars) in 2020, up 31.1% year on year. Over the past five years, China's cross-border e-commerce has grown nearly tenfold.

Within this context, Statista's Digital Market Outlook (2021) provides a wide overview on the Chinese fashion e-commerce market, including the sale of physical goods via a digital channel to a private end user (B2C). Purchases via desktop computer (including notebooks and laptops), as well as purchases via mobile devices such as smartphones and tablets, present a significant rise forecasted from 2020 to 2025. For example, the apparel segment's online revenue in China is expected to grow from its current 177.356,6 to 285.981,4 million U.S. dollars in 2025.

Since February 2020, several Chinese and Western luxury brands have opened flagship stores on Tmall Luxury Pavilion, a website launched in 2017 by Alibaba. Tmall Luxury is China's leading online destination for high-end and designer brands. The portal announced new features to bolster luxury brands' connections with China's Gen Z, a digital-first fashion-forward customer base that is fast becoming a driver of global luxury consumption.

Tmall Luxury launched three new features to educate, entertain, and engage a new generation of luxury buyers as its core business audience: Soho Live, a daily live-streaming service focusing on all things luxury; Soho Mag, a content-rich channel with the latest fashion news, jointly developed with fashion editors and trend-setting influencers; and an upgraded membership program offering personalized services to high-value customers. Around 80% of the customers on the platform are 35 years of old or younger, with the highest concentration in the 26–30 age group. With the number of luxury consumers in the 18–25 age group more than doubling between July 2018 and June 2019, this young consumer segment is set to become an even bigger driver in the luxury industry (Alibaba Group, 2020).

By 2020, Chinese social media use was estimated to hit 647 million active users, resulting in a dramatic change of the consumers' behavior and, consequently, in the strategies companies adopt when dealing with the Chinese market. Many international brands have experimented with social media, such as Xiaohongshu, using live streaming, digital store integration, and gaming. According to Statista, as of July 2019, the platform had a total of approximately 300 million registered users, after tripling three times over since mid-2018. Around 35% of users were between 31 and 35 years old, and around 85% of users were female. Anna Tolette, a content marketing associate at Synthesio, says: "The *Xiahongshu* experience supports all aspects of these new consumer dynamics. To know and succeed with *Xiaohongshu* (Wei & Banjo, 2019) is to know and succeed with China's new and ever-evolving purchasing behaviors" (thedrum.com, 2020). Xiaohongshu, much like Instagram, is a lifestyle platform that has the ability to create hot topics. However, the platform is different in that users create and interact with longer, blog-style reviews of products. Chinese consumers rely heavily on reviews and testimonials from friends, family, and Key Opinion Leaders (KOLs). Xiaohongshu has provided a platform for this type of discussion.

2020, the year the COVID-19 pandemic began worldwide, marked a significant turning point in digitalization in fashion. The most significant proof of this turning point is the digitalization of several important fashion weeks. For example, Paris Fashion Week and Milan Fashion Week—the most important fashion business appointments worldwide—have digitalized their shows and forums through online hubs using marketing and data analysis platforms or live broadcasting around the world in collaboration with international media partners (Yun & Ko, 2021). In Asia, renowned fashion weeks implemented the most consistent steps forward. Seoul Fashion Week developed a special service for fashion buyers through a B2B online platform, as well as a communication platform with Chinese consumers using WeChat mini-programs. Tokyo Fashion Week used the digital platform Joor to present the shows, which were connected to virtual look-books and services for buyers.

Thus, 2020 represented a significant milestone for fashion, not only from the point of view of design, production, and sales methods but also related to communication and relationships with consumers. Before 2020, these elements were consolidated, reassuring, and manageable, while after the context was uncertain, unstable, and constantly evolving. The social distancing imposed by the pandemic has thus defined a new communicative "normality," which takes on ever-changing forms that do not necessarily replace the previous performing ways, but which sublimate and amplify what can be considered as the traditional communicative tools of fashion, such as in-person fashion shows (Linfante & Pompa, 2021).

Shanghai Digital Fashion Week represented the most significant event within this new digital landscape. On March 24, 2020, the 2020 Shanghai Fashion Week opened in live-streaming format and was held for the first time as a Digital Fashion Week. Shanghai Fashion Week, along with Alibaba Group, intended to demonstrate how innovative technologies can be combined with fashion. During the event, fashion shows of about 150 brands and designers were broadcast through the online shopping mall Tmall, the open market Taobao Live, and on social media. China made the first attempt to release the entire fashion week digitally. During fashion week in March, online sales amounted to 500 million yuan, or $7.2 million, and more than 6 million people accessed Digital Fashion Week on the first day alone, with a cumulative number of views over 11 million (Alizia, 2020) (Fig. 6).

While the virtual runway has made exclusive fashion events more accessible to the public, it has also opened up new possibilities for designers to interact directly with their consumers. For example, 2020 China Fashion Week collaborated with Chinese short-video platform Douyin's e-commerce department to present the latest in fashion to audiences both online and offline. Youci is a rising star in China's accessories scene, and the brand is making good use of the Douyin live-streaming platforms to expand its reach. As Zhang Jiajie, the designer at Youci, told CGTN: "We

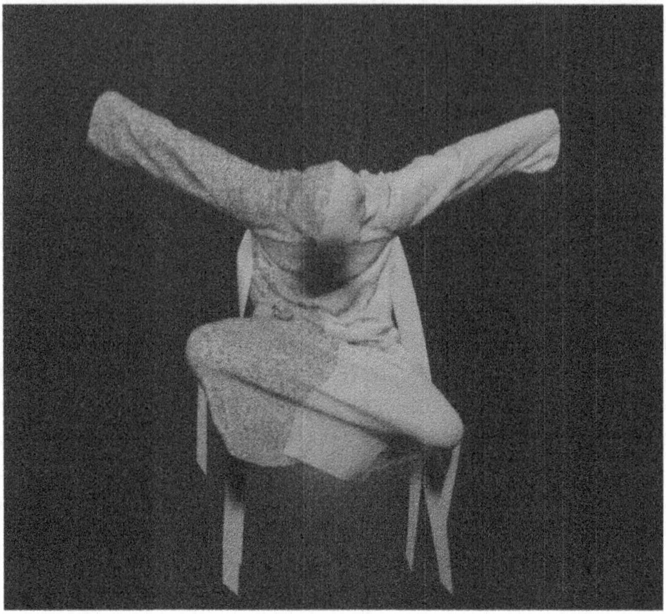

**Fig. 6** Digital fashion item (*Source* Metamorphic Fashion research University of Florence, Italy)

are taking part in this year's event both on and off line. During the day, we present our products at the Designer Hub Showroom. And at night, we turn to livestreams on Douyin" (Lin, 2021). He continues: "Since we are a relatively new brand, and this is our first attempt live-streaming on Douyin, it helps more consumers on Douyin to learn about us" (Lin, 2021). Zhao Huizhou, the founder of Eachway, a homegrown Chinese brand, says that learning how to verbalize her design concepts is important during these online presentations: "When I present my works on the catwalk, people's focus is on the clothes [...] but when it's delivered online, it's more about the stories in designing them [...] So through live-streaming, we share with consumers the visions we hold for our designs [...] it's a direct way of communication" (Lin, 2021).

## 6 Successful Screen-Based Case Studies in China: The Dominance of Visceral Playful Emotions

According to what has been laid out in previous sections, mediatization offers significant new spaces to tap into consumers' feelings and sensibilities. Thus, brand and product storytelling cover a significant role in market positioning and competitiveness.

Since 2019 we can highlight significant case studies of interactive screen-based UX related to e-commerce platforms, social media, or apps, in particular in the high-end fashion market. The fashion business involves not only designing clothing and accessories but also furthermore engages in styling strategies and product presentations. The Covid pandemic has significantly strengthened market mediatization, generating some effective communication and fashion campaigns. Within this digitalized context, emotions play an important role. Emotional responses could be tied directly to the device itself or also influenced by contextual factors. Controllable aspects of interactive experiences deeply relate to clear patterns of emotion in the responses of the users.

We can highlight recurrent characteristics of the most successful fashion styling and communication campaigns. First of all, the most popular digital campaigns, often managed by leading international fashion brands, focus on styling strategies and special design output through a "transcendent" approach, discarding at all the "immanent" values of the design collections and their technical real qualities (Castelli, 2000). In fact, we notice an increased cost and importance of activities that deal with intangibles, such as fashion trends, brand identities, design, and innovation, over activities that deal with tangibles, including the transformation, manipulation, and movement of physical goods. As intangibles become more important, tangibles have become increasingly commodified (Gereffi et al., 2001). Within this transformation, thanks to committed leadership in ICT and the technological device industry, China represents a one-of-a-kind example in the international market that we will explore in this section.

In China, fashion mediatization usually avoids any specific information and storytelling about complex values as qualities of the artifact; therefore, the screen-based user experience is a pillar of user engagement and entertainment. Chinese brands propose a hedonic "*wow effect*" that distracts and entertains the consumer, without engaging them with the intrinsic values of the artifact and the brand. These mediatic strategies lead to specific "pitfalls" of communication, as these brands often underestimate key values related to the aura of product and any synesthetic experience with the fashion item (Fry et al., 2017). As a result, the marketing campaigns of the leading corporations stress the visceral and behavioral emotional levels of the interaction, completely discarding the reflective one intended with other approaches to marketing (Fig. 7).

The hedonic playful campaigns presented by the Gucci Doraemon capsule are perfectly in line with this trend. In the campaigns, a retro-style video game language entertains the user. Gucci strongly targets Millennials and Gen Z users in China without introducing Chinese users to the history of the brand and the reasons why Gucci has become a globally renowned brand. Gucci recruited photographer Angelo Pennetta to

**Fig. 7** Shop window in Nanjing City (*Photo* Gabriele Goretti)

shoot an accompanying campaign before the line of apparel and accessories launched ahead of Chinese New Year 2019. The imagery presents a hybrid of Doraemon's signature whimsy and Gucci's hyper-decorative luxury sensibility.

Doraemon is the star of the show, as the Japanese animated icon lounges, laughs, and indulges alongside a collective of stylish Gucci models draped in the collaborative garments while toting complementary bags, scarves, and sneakers. The latter includes some accessories realized with illustrative Doraemon motifs atop Gucci monogrammed patterns, with various matching iPhone cases, canvas wallets, and bags. The all-over design is also characterized by lush dresses, jackets, skirts, shirts, and tracksuits crafted from jersey and silk alike, reinforcing the retro louche aesthetic that has become Gucci's signature. Other ready-to-wear styles include intarsia knit sweaters, interlocking GG T-shirts, denim shorts, and a leather-trimmed bucket hat.

Other fashion brands have developed a real videogame-based language to entertain young Chinese users. *Honor of Kings* (王者荣耀) is among the biggest games in the world, and among the most fashionable as well. Tencent-owned developer TiMi Studios collaborated with fashion house Burberry on new character skins. The skins were designed by Riccardo Tisci, chief creative officer at Burberry, for the character Yao: "Burberry's signature gabardine, pioneered by founder Thomas Burberry and designed to protect the wearer against the elements, fits seamlessly with Yao, who personifies the role of a protector for her teammates" (store.steampowered.com, 2021). The two skins, designed with the "spirit of nature" in mind, will be available for players to purchase in mainland China, although there's no word on a release date. The competitive multiplayer game for mobile devices has become so popular that Tencent has had to impose daily limits on players in the past; the developer says *Honor of Kings* averaged 100 million daily players during November 2020.

The big payoff from Chinese online gaming for luxury brands is its huge and still growing group of young, mainly female Chinese players. Their age group also represents one of the biggest spenders on luxury goods in China. A 2017 research report from Tencent Institute on Games shows that the popular multiplayer online battle arena game *Honor of Kings* had collected over 100 million female users, which represented 54% of the total players of the game, while more than 52% of users were below the age of 24, according to TalkingData (Peng, 2019).

Other Western luxury brands have not invested as much as Gucci, Burberry, or LVMH group in mediatization, and their growth has been quite poor as a result. The Chinese Millennials that are driving sales growth in luxury fashion on the mainland live their fashion experiences and purchases on social media. There they follow and connect with brands on the hunt for new status symbols.

Prada's strategy is one of the most significant case studies of a brand that has made very limited investments in playful, fancy, digital communication. In March 2019, Jing Daily spoke with a few Chinese luxury shoppers about Prada. "I feel Prada is not in vogue," one said. In addition, Prada is not a leading player in the Chinese fashion market because of the values and imaginary the company offers. The brand is strongly connected to artistic and intellectual references that are quite complex and related to Western history and imaginaries. The complexity of Prada's contents and values is not easily transferable to the rising Millennial audience in China.

The Prada brand launched a new Chinese e-commerce site in December 2017, alongside a new media campaign. Prada launched a series of experimental initiatives named "Feels Like Prada" in several worldwide cities to promote its Fall/Winter 2021 campaign. Rong Zhai, the brand's social and cultural hub in Shanghai, and a fruit and vegetable market located in the Wulumuqi Road neighborhood of the city, were transformed by Prada with its iconic codes and prints from the new collection. On Xiaohongshu, over 250 users posted about the Prada market in the 12 hours after it opened to the public. Visitors were highly impressed by this creative initiative that employs the identity of this everyday space; local fashionistas holding vegetables or flowers with Prada packaging have become "Instagrammable" moments on social platforms. Prada's unexpected takeover impressed local young audiences and drew many of them to visit this market and feel the brand vibrantly and emotionally.

## 7 Potentials of Reflective Emotions in China's High-End Market

Despite the massive mediatization process, we have explored above in relation to China's high-end fashion market, we can highlight some emerging potential. The "lean-forward" moments where digital content is consumed during waiting moments and long transport rides are rising as a new way to structure user experiences. WeChat mini-programs and other kinds of entertaining media can represent an effective way to structure new presentations of products' values and brand intangible assets. Moreover, the previously mentioned "lean-back" user scenarios could stand as a strategic way to define new meaningful user digital journeys. Articles of two pages or more or a mini-program on WeChat could be developed to focus on significant aspects and intrinsic values of products that cannot be explained through quick "*wow effect*" and fast gaming-based interactions.

According to this perspective, the rising interest of Chinese segments of customers in fashion products' sustainability and inner values (such as "made in," authenticity, and traceability) can offer new opportunities to include significant reflective emotions in playful experiences. In addition, the digitalization of the supply chain and new generative design opportunities can put the customer-based interaction even more at the center of fashion business. By focusing more on the "activation" and "guidance" sides of the playful experience, rather than just focusing on the euphoric elements, it is possible to develop new user journeys based on their evolving fashion values.

According to Resnick (2014), game design users, as digital natives and digital consumers, can experience reflective interactions (as digital citizens) through a deeper understanding of digital contents and through becoming digital contributors. However, this proactive attitude alone is not sufficient in a learning process or in a field practice. This must be supported by the more retrospective process of reflection; therefore, one suggestion is to implement strategies that involve users, such as "reflection-on-games." Reflection-on-games helps users to articulate conceptual knowledge on game programming and game design. In the retrospective reflection process, users' own experiences are connected to emerging conceptual knowledge (Majgaard, 2014). Following this perspective, it is possible to generate new immersive reflective emotions through playful meaningful interactions and game design strategies, not only creating quick hedonic exciting effects, but structuring *knowledge-in-interaction* processes that can drive the user to connect with deeper intrinsic values.

Within this emerging combination of playful digital experiences and reflective emotions, we can refer to four activity principles (Van der Meij et al., 2017): narration, imagination, action-reflection, and co-creation. Depending on the aims of learning and reflection, these activity principles can be applied individually or in combination with one another. The effect of *narration* on learning is engagement by empathy, since the narratives invite learners to step in the shoes of others and take on a temporary perspective that is different from their own. In this way, the content of the learning and reflection process becomes more personal to them. We, therefore, argue that narratives increase learners' degrees of engagement with, and sometimes even respect for, other perspectives (Van der Meij et al., 2017).

According to Cheng (2011), *imagination* introduces brainstorming and creative modes for thinking about the unknown or wondering about new scenarios. This reflective principle opens up a dreaming stage, allowing individuals to figure out different conditions and contexts. An additional factor of reflective experience is *action-reflection* principle, which facilitates consequential thinking during the learning and reflection: learners juxtapose the familiar and unfamiliar, discover the different effects of actions (Rogers & Price, 2004), or discover actual actions and reactions as a consequence of pre-conceived thinking (Caci et al., 2013).

Moreover, the key usefulness of collaboration for *co-creation* in playful learning may lie in Kangas' (2010) socio-cultural vision of learning: in social processes, people tend to first learn inter-mentally and thereafter intra-mentally. In other words, the collaborative tackling of something completely new in order to reach a particular, commonly agreed-upon tangible goal requires negotiation of different minds within which individual learning also implicitly takes place. As consequence of the four previous principles, *experimentation* allows the user to discover new opportunities, solutions, or interactions (Caci et al., 2013). In other words, a large experimentation space supports the creation of a multitude of diverging thoughts and actions.

To allow the user to investigate and explore new interaction fields, learners need small and comprehensible tasks or topics to facilitate a deeper reflection on specific topics (Kangas, 2010). In other words, relatively small tasks and content give learners greater opportunity and time to *focus* on these issues, yielding deeper learning but also facilitating reflection on broader issues. In the end, the effect of *stimulating guidance* lies in increased motivation and engagement of learners throughout the whole learning process (Lin, 2010).

Within the scope of Western fashion, Brunello Cucinelli is a representative brand that aims at developing "lateral thinking" in the fashion user experience, both digitally and physically. The Italian brand was founded as SME in 1978 in the medieval hamlet of Solomeo, a small hilltop village located on the outskirts of Perugia (Umbria, Italy); the brand specializes in cashmere. Brunello Cucinelli's success derives from the concept of the "humanistic enterprise model" (Del Baldo, 2020), whose foundations are (1) excellence in craftsmanship and manual skills; (2) authentic "Made in Italy" labeling as a connection between past and future technology; and (3) the dignity of work, profit, and a special relationship with the surrounding territory outside of Solomeo (Del Baldo, 2020). The company is engaged in the development of communication language for netizens, which could be a crucial key point to marketing in China. The attention on Solomeo, a village centered around quality and social/eco sustainability, as well as a focus on the craftsmanship aura in the village, narrates the supply chain of the products in a way that has the potential to involve digital fashion users in those complex values.

The rising attention from the Chinese fashion system on intangible cultural heritage and ethnic minorities' know-how drives similar complex meanings and narrations within China. For example, Dejin, a fashion brand by designer Zhou Li, launched its 2022 Spring/Summer collection at China Fashion Week (China Daily, 2021). The line's textiles integrated characters of the Naxi people from Southwest China's Yunnan province using embroidery techniques from East China's Shandong province. Exquisite ornaments in jade, some dating back to the Ming (1368–1644) and Qing (1636–1912) dynasties, decorate the garments and embody auspicious hopes for the future, as well as deep ties to the past.

Understanding and rediscovering intangible cultural values in contemporary fashion is not just a matter of styling. Visceral emotions are usually entertaining and reminders of an historical topic in a quick and fancy way that is often quite superficial. Reflective paths in digital UX can allow the user to understand their involvement in cultural values through those historical decorations. This exchange of contents and emotions between the brand and the audience allows for new playful fidelization processes developed by streaming content and interactive platforms.

An interesting path on craftsmanship rituals and intangible cultural heritage is also offered by the brand First Flag, based in Suzhou. First

Flag[3] is a brand of knit items that have leveraged the delicate handwork of Suzhou, China, known for its embroidery.[4] The warm and rich soil has nurtured colorful culture and rich traditional handicrafts. Among them, the "Crown of Splendid Embroidery," a craftsmanship tradition referring to Song Jin and Su Embroidery, represents the highest level of handmade fabric craftsmanship. During the Ming and Qing dynasties, Suzhou became the most prosperous center of the weaving industry. A large number of exquisite and luxurious handmade fabrics were exported from Suzhou to countries all over the world through the Silk Road.

The brand offers Chinese-style children's clothes whose silk and cotton materials are chosen carefully to reflect world-class quality. Going beyond mere functionality, the company proposes the idea of "festival garb," which combines China's art of exquisite hand knitting with high quality materials. Incorporating the handicrafts of weaving and embroidering typical of Suzhou represents a strategic value for the brand.

The brand stands as a significant example of new generations of Chinese high-end fashion projects and quality artifacts, including tangible and intangible values from the vast Chinese intangible cultural heritage. The brand's mission relates to "styling" playful experiences by referring to Chinese history while focusing on rediscovering the rituals of embroidery savoir-faire, the beauty of raw materials, and fascination with the Suzhou genius loci. Within this new wave of Chinese fashion projects relating to the aura of artisanship, digital experiences are being incorporated that involve and inform the user about the charming "fancy" cultural journey they are a part of when they purchase these brands (Fig. 8).

## 8 Conclusion

More than ever, consumption is connected with emotions, which means that we can decide what we need according to both tangible and intangible needs. It also demonstrates that our needs as consumers have expanded from largely material things to include spiritual and social needs.

Emotional consumption is an economic activity that is affected by the social environment. In China, as well as other parts of the world,

[3] https://www.firstflagkids.com.

[4] Suzhou is an ancient city in the south of the Yangtze River. The lush scenery surrounded by mountains and rivers has made it known as "paradise on earth."

**Fig. 8** Silkworms within brocade craftsmanship exhibition at Nanjing Silk Museum (*Photo* Gabriele Goretti)

people's consumer behaviors have begun to transform from simple material enjoyment to "spiritual" leisure, from tangible demand satisfaction to intangible demand satisfaction. The costumers pay for feelings, and for intense feelings even more so. In the context of China, it reflects netizens' changing expressions of freedom and personality that have been rapidly developing in China in recent years. According to this emerging scenario, we can highlight new challenges in communication and design strategies both for established brands and new creative projects.

As reported in McKinsey Megatrends 2021 (Bu et al., 2021), we can highlight emerging fictional stories of people living in virtual reality worlds that, on the other hand, are rapidly transitioning into "real world" values. Chinese consumers are moving more and more of their social interactions and leisure activities into virtual domains, but they are looking more and more to develop consistent values related to real matters. Virtual and physical social activities are then merging as presented in the new "digital era" of fashion shows, where visionary videos and references to real products are re-mixed. Thus, the digitalization of manufacturing processes and the integration of new digital services reflect the new role of reflective emotions, which could play a significant role in understanding and experiencing new imaginaries of fashion.

## References


Aftab, M., & Rusli, H. A. (2017). Designing visceral, behavioural and reflective products. *Chinese Journal of Mechanical Engineering, 30*(5), 1058–1068.

Alibaba Group. (2020). *Tmall luxury connects high-end brands with China's "New luxury" Gen Z consumers*. https://www.alibabagroup.com/en/news/article?news=p200825

Alizia Group. (2020). *What shanghai's first digital fashion week meant for brands and designers*. https://www.alizila.com/what-shanghais-first-digital-fashion-week-meant-for-brands-and-designers/

Anderson, K. C., Knight, D. K., Pookulangara, S., & Josiam, B. M. (2014). Influence of hedonic and utilitarian motivations on retailer loyalty and purchase intention: A Facebook perspective. *Journal of Retailing and Consumer Services, 21*, 773–779. https://doi.org/10.1016/j.retconser.2014.05.007

Avery Dennison Report. (2017). Digital emotional intelligence. *A customer experience framework to understand and anticipate human emotion across physical and digital channels*. https://rbis.averydennison.com/content/dam/averydennison/rbis/global/apparel/Documents/Avery-Dennison-Digital-Emotional-Intelligence.pdf

Azoya International. (2020). *The WeChat mini-program playbook for E-commerce 2021* (Azoya Group Report). https://www.azoyagroup.com/resources/view/the-wechat-mini-program-playbook-for-e-commerce-2021/

Babin, B. J., Darden, W. R., & Griffin, M. (1994). Work and/or fun: Measuring hedonic and utilitarian shopping value. *Journal of Consumer Research, 20*(4), 644–656. https://doi.org/10.1086/209376

Bu, L., Chung, V., Leung, N., Wang, W. L., Xia, B., & Xia, C. (2021). *The future of digital innovation in China: Megatrends shaping one of the world's fastest evolving digital ecosystems*. McKinsey. https://www.mckinsey.com/featured-insights/china/the-future-of-digital-innovation-in-china-megatrends-shaping-one-of-the-worlds-fastest-evolving-digital-ecosystems

Caci, B., Chiazzese, G., & D'Amico, A. (2013). Robotic and virtual world programming labs to stimulate reasoning and visual-spatial abilities. *Procedia: Social & Behavioral Sciences, 93*, 1493–1497.

Castelli, C. T. (2000). *Transitive design, a design language for the zeroes*. Electa.

Cheng, C. Y. (2011). Interpreting paradigm of change in Chinese philosophy. *Journal of Chinese Philosophy, 38*(3), 339–367.

China Academy of Information and Communications Technologies (CAICT). (2020). *Digital economy development in China*. http://www.caict.ac.cn/english/research/whitepapers/202007/P020200728343679920779.pdf

China Daily. (2021, September 10). Chinese cultural heritage shines at China Fashion Week. *China Daily*. Retrieved from https://www.chinadaily.com.cn/a/202109/10/WS613b0af3a310efa1bd66eafe.html

China Entertainment and Media Outlook in China (2016–2020). *PWC*. https://www.pwccn.com/en/entertainment-media/em-china-outlook-nov2016.pdf

China Mobile Internet. (2013). *Overview, Umeng insight report*, March 2014.

Del Baldo, M. (2020). *Company case study 8: Cucinelli-A humanistic enterprise for a sustainable growth and a sustainable world*. http://hdl.handle.net/11576/2681232

Derks, D., Fisher, A. H., & Bros, A. E. R. (2008). The role of emotion in computer-mediated communication: A review. *Computers in Human Behavior, 24*(3), 766–785.

Desmet, P., & Hekkert, P. (2007). Framework of product experience. *Journal of Design, 1*(1), 57–66.

Evans, C. (2003). *Fashion at the edge: Spectacle, modernity and deathliness*. Yale University Press.

Fashionchinaagency.com. (2021). *How luxury brands reach Chinese millennials with digital*. Fashion China Agency. https://fashionchinaagency.com/how-luxury-brands-reach-chinese-millenials-with-digital/

Findlay, R. (2015). The short, passionate and close-knit history of personal style blogs. *Fashion Theory: The Journal of Dress, Body and Culture, 19*(2), 157–178.

Fry, A., Goretti, G., Ladhib, S., Cianfanelli, E., & Overby, C. (2017). Advanced craft integrated with saper fare. The role of intangible values and the centrality of the artisan in high-quality 21st century artisanship. *Cuaderno Journal, Emerging Processes in Design Practice and Design Education, 64*(18), 255–276.

Geng, L., & Li, X. (2018). An empirical study on the relationship between consumption emotions and brand loyalty. *Chinese Journal of Communication, 11*(3), 267–288. https://doi.org/10.1080/17544750.2018.1445118

Gereffi, G., Humphrey, J., Kaplinsky, R., & Sturgeon, T. J. (2001). Introduction: Globalization, value chains and development. *IDS Bulletin, 32*(3).

GMA. (2021). *How luxury brands reach Chinese millennials with digital*. Fashion Agency. https://fashionchinaagency.com/how-luxury-brands-reach-chinese-millenials-with-digital/

Goretti, G., Terenzi, B., Cianfanelli, E., Crescenzi, P., Colombo, C., & Civitelli, E. (2020). A phygital approach to playful experience in learning processes for kids with special educational needs. *ICETC'20: 12th International Conference on Education Technology and Computers* (pp. 223–229).

Greeven, M. J. (2004). *The evolution of high-technology in China after 1978: Towards technological entrepreneurship*. ERIM.

Hu, C., & Tan, L. (2020). Fast fashion and sustainability amongst Chinese millennials. In J. E. Richard & D. Kadirov (Eds.), *ANMAC 2019 Wind of Change Conference Proceedings* (p. 1359). https://researchers.mq.edu.au/en/publications/fast-fashion-and-sustainability-amongst-chinese-millennials

International Trade Center. (2016). *E-Commerce in China opportunities for Asian firms*. AliResearch.

Jingting, Z. (2019). Emotions and consumption of the netizens in China's digital economy. *Revista Latinoamericana De Estudios Sobre Cuerpos, Emociones y Sociedad, 11*(30), 89–98.

Kangas, M. (2010). Creative and playful learning: Learning through game co-creation and games in a playful learning environment. *Thinking Skills and Creativity, 1*(5), 1–15.

Keane, M. A. (2004). Brave new world: Understanding China's creative vision. *International Journal of Cultural Policy, 10*(3), 265–279.

Kramer, A. D. I., Guillory, J. E., & Hancock, J. T. (2014). Experimental evidence of massive-scale emotional contagion through social networks. *Proceedings of the National Academy of Sciences, 111*, 8788–8790. https://doi.org/10.1073/pnas.1320040111

Lessig, L. (2008). *Remix: Making art and commerce thrive in the hybrid economy*. Penguin Press.

Lim, S. (2020). Emerging platforms: What is Xiaohongshu and how can brands leverage it? *The Drum*. https://www.thedrum.com/news/2020/03/16/emerging-platforms-what-xiaohongshu-and-how-can-brands-leverage-it

Lin, L. (2010). The relationship of consumer personality trait, brand personality and brand loyalty: An empirical study of toys and video games buyers. *Journal of Product & Brand Management*.

Lin, L. (2021, March 31). *China Fashion Week: Fashion digitization, an industry gamechanger*. CGTN. https://news.cgtn.com/news/2021-03-31/China-Fashion-Week-Fashion-digitization-an-industry-gamechanger-Z4G3hmFcCA/index.html

Lindgren, T. (2014). Fashion system Shanghai: The advent of a new gatekeeper. In J. L. Foltyn & R. Fisher (Eds.), *Proceedings of 5th Global Conference: Fashion—Exploring Critical Issues* (pp. 1–8). Inter-Disciplinary.Net.

Linfante, V., & Pompa, C. (2021). Space, time and catwalks: Fashion shows as a multilayered communication channel. *ZoneModa Journal, 11*(1), 15–42.

Liu, Z., & Song, G. (2018). The influence of smartphone on the change of lifestyle [智 能手机与生活方式变迁及其影响]. *Studies in Philosophy of Science and Technology, 35*(1), 111–116.

Lotto, B. (2017). Enhancing human attachment: Digital emotions. In A. Dennison (Ed.), *Digital emotional intelligence, a customer experience framework to understand and anticipate human emotion across physical and digital channels.*

Ma, W. (2017). *Digital economy 2.0* (Chinese). Wiley.

Majgaard, G. (2014). The playful and reflective game designer. *Electronic Journal of E-Learning, 12*(3), 271–280.

McKinsey Institute. (2017). *Chinese luxury consumers: More global, more demanding, still spending*. https://www.mckinsey.com/business-functions/growth-marketing-and-sales/our-insights/chinese-luxury-consumers-more-global-more-demanding-still-spending

Mckinsey Institute. (2021). *The state of fashion 2021 report*. McKinsey Institute. https://www.mckinsey.com/~/media/mckinsey/industries/retail/our%20insights/state%20of%20fashion/2021/the-state-of-fashion-2021-vf.pdf

Menkes, S. (2010, May 18). Fashion films become the hottest new accessories. *The New York Times*. https://www.nytimes.com/2010/05/18/fashion/18iht-fcurves.html

Norman, D. A. (2005). *Emotional design: Why we love (or hate) everyday things*. Basic Books.

O'Kelly, R., Rosberg, M., Walsh, D., & Davis, J. (2021). *Striving to sustain returns. How wholesale banks can unlock hidden value*. In Oliver Wyman Report 2021. https://www.oliverwyman.com/our-expertise/insights/2021/apr/wholesale-investment-banks-analysis-2021.html

Pan, Y. (2019). Prada's problems in China are deeper than the economic slowdown. *Jing Daily-The Business of Luxury in China*. https://jingdaily.com/prada-problem-china/

Park, S. C. (2014). Ichpedia: A case study in community engagement in the safeguarding of ICH online. *International Journal of Intangible Heritage, 9*, 71–84.

Peng, Z. (2019). Why luxury brands should care about online gaming in China. *Jing Daily-The Business of Luxury in China*. https://jingdaily.com/why-luxury-brands-should-care-about-online-gaming-in-china/

Piek, H. (2008). *Technology development in rural industries: A study of China's collectives*. Practical Actions Publishing.

Prunesti, A. (2016). *Social media e comunicazione di marketing. Presidiare la Rete, costruire relazioni e acquisire clienti innovando l'esperienza utente* [Social media and marketing communication: Manning internet networks, building relations and acquiring new customer by innovating on the user experience]. Franco Angeli.

Resnick, M. (2014). *Learn gamification for iOS development: Adding game elements to other types of apps*. Apress

Rocamora, A. (2016). Mediatization and digital media in the field of fashion. *Fashion Theory: The Journal of Dress, Body and Culture, 21*(5), 505–522.
Rogers, Y., & Price, S. (2004). *The role of mobile devices in facilitating collaborative inquiry in situ*. World Scientific Publishing Company & Asia-Pacific Society for Computers in Education.
Silbert, J. (2021). Doraemon pals around with Gucci models in collaborative lookbook. *Hypebeast*. https://hypebeast.com/2021/1/doraemon-gucci-chinese-new-year-collection-campaign
Smith, T. (2019). Do Chinese consumers care about sustainable fashion? *Jing Daily-The Business of Luxury in China*. https://jingdaily.com/do-chinese-consumers-care-about-sustainable-fashion/
Song, J., & Qu, H. (2018). How does consumer regulatory focus impact perceived value and consumption emotions? *International Journal of Contemporary Hospitality Management, 31*(1), 285–308.
Statista. (2021). *Digital market outlook*. https://www.statista.com/outlook/digital-markets
Statistical Report on Internet Development in China—CNNIC. (2014). *China Internet Network Information Center*. https://www.cnnic.com.cn/IDR/ReportDownloads/201411/P020141102574314897888.pdf
Suen, Z. (2021). *Three ways brands are tapping China's digitally native luxury shoppers*. Business of Fashion. https://www.businessoffashion.com/briefings/china/three-ways-brands-are-tapping-chinas-digitally-native-luxury-shoppers
Sun, Y., Wang, R., Cao, D., & Lee, R. (2021). Who are social media influencers for luxury fashion consumption of the Chinese Gen Z? Categorisation and empirical examination. *Journal of Fashion Marketing and Management*. https://doi.org/10.1108/JFMM-07-2020-0132
Tidrick, G. (1986). *Productivity, growth, and technological change in Chinese industry* (World Bank Staff Working Paper No. 761).
Tong, J. (2015). The formation of an agonistic public sphere: Emotions, the Internet and news media in China. *China Information, 29*(3), 333–351.
Uhlirova, M. (2013). 100 years of the fashion film: Frameworks and histories. *Fashion Theory, 17*(2), 137–157.
Van der Meij, M. G., Broerse, J. E. W., & Kupper, F. (2017). Conceptualizing playfulness for reflection processes in responsible research and innovation contexts: A narrative literature review. *Journal of Responsible Innovation, 4*(1), 43–63.
Walther, J. B. (1992). Interpersonal effects in computer-mediated interaction: A relational perspective. *Communication Research, 19*(1), 52–90.
Wang, B. (2017). *Chinese visions of world order: Tianxia, culture, and world politics*. Duke University Press.

Webster, A. (2021, March 22). Burberry designed character skins for China's biggest video game. *The Verge*. https://www.theverge.com/2021/3/22/22340775/honor-of-kings-burberry-skin-fashion-video-games

Wei, D. & Banjo, S. (24 April 2019). *The future of shopping is already happening in China: China's Gen z skips the stores and shops on social media*. Bloomberg. https://www.bloomberg.com/news/articles/2019-04-24/china-s-gen-z-skips-the-stores-and-shops-on-social-media

Williams, K. A. (2014). Recut film trailers, nostalgia and the teen film. In K. M. Baton & J. M. Lampley (Eds.), *Fan Culture: Essays on participatory fandom in the 21st century* (pp. 47–60). McFarland & Co.

Xiaojuan, J. (1997). Chinese government policy towards science and technology and its influence on the technical development of industrial enterprises. In *Chinese cultural transfer in the 1990's: Current experiences, historical problems and international perspectives*. Edward Edgar.

Xiaoyi, L. (2020). Retro fashions: Recycling used clothing: A trend in China. *Global Times*. https://www.globaltimes.cn/content/1204277.shtml

Yun, H., & Ko, E. (2021). Comparative analysis of seven digital fashion weeks. *Journal of Fashion Business, 25*(3), 36–50.

Zhang, D. (2019). *How Chinese internet celebrity influences consumer attitude to purchase on e-commerce*. Uppsala Univesriteit.

Zhijun, L. (2016). Consumption of emotions. *Chinese Clothes, 9*, 100–101.

CHAPTER 6

# Shanghai Fashion and Post-1990s Youth Through the Phygital Lens

*Sabine Chrétien-Ichikawa*

## 1 Foreword

After a career as a designer and manager in the fashion industry in Europe, the USA, and Japan, I started doing research on the history of the fashion industry globally. In this endeavor, Florida's (2003) concept of the creative class, Breward and Gilbert's (2006) analysis of fashion capitals, Rocamora's (2009) study of media and fashion cities, and Kawamura's (2004) explanation of fashion institutionalization influenced my questioning as I sought to explore the emergence of China's fashion creativity. When I first went to China in 2005 as a visiting scholar, my encounter with the city of Shanghai changed my vision of world fashion. Considering the current situation, I count myself lucky to witness first-hand the transformation of Shanghai city into a potential epicenter of fashion creation, in the last ten years. Chinese fashion is still an emerging

S. Chrétien-Ichikawa (✉)
ESSCA School of Management, Shanghai, China
e-mail: sabine.ichikawa@essca.fr



S. Chrétien-Ichikawa and K. Pawlik (eds.), *Creative Industries and Digital Transformation in China*,
https://doi.org/10.1007/978-981-19-3049-2_6

topic in both business and academic circles. But it offers a chance to study a creative industry "in the making" (Chrétien-Ichikawa, 2015), which intrigued me for the potential historical perspective it offered. I was drawn to situate the city's rise by comparing it with mature fashion capitals like Paris, Milan, and Tokyo. Moreover, Shanghai was instrumental in the drive to widen my scope to explore the origins of fashion creativity I had previously taken for granted.

The empirical findings presented in this chapter are excerpts of ongoing and broader research on Chinese fashion started around 2005. My observations are based on combining some 200 interviews with entrepreneurs, designers, youth, and institutions related to fashion, with constant field observations in Shanghai and online content scanning. It allowed me to analyze the birth of a new fashion system. Researching Chinese fashion is relevant to world viewers because both the market and consumers are evolving rapidly, offering a sea of opportunities to foreign fashion players. However, I do not examine China simply as a market but rather focus on it as a novel source of creativity. I observe the emergence of what constitutes a unique ecosystem, comparing it with other cultures and economic contexts. As such, this chapter highlights the influence of technology on the post-1990s generation, who are perhaps the first generation to be both creators and consumers of fashion on a wide scale.

## 2 Introduction: Why Youth, Fashion, and Technology?

Fashion studies examine the production, diffusion, and distribution of fashion, and the wider context of its institutions, consumption, and culture. Transforming a functional item of clothing into intangible fashion requires cultural and institutional mediation (Craik, 2003; Kawamura, 2004). The mechanisms that ascribe symbolic value to fashion can be observed in sociocultural elements, and in metropolises. As a matter of fact, the use of the term "Made in Shanghai" has increased in the last few years, to distinguish items originating in Shanghai from the global image of a mass-produced "Made in China" label. Therefore, the study of fashion in this particular city bears specific significance.

Studying youth and technology is not new in fashion studies.[1] Fashion sociologist Kawamura (2004) examined this topic in the West and in Japan. Scholarship on Chinese youth (Liu, 2011), and on Chinese fashion in particular, is still scarce, as is research exploring the relationship between youth and technology. Fashion scholars have contributed to my understanding of the Chinese fashion history and industry (Finnane, 2008; Lindgren, 2013; Ling & Segre-Reinach, 2018; Tsui, 2013a, 2017), but they have not studied the impact of technology on youth and fashion. This study helps to fill this gap.

The next question is: Why study young people's aspirations in relation to fashion? Anthropologist Appadurai (2004) pointed out that aspirations are not only individual, but they are formed in interaction with social life. Hence it is important to understand the environment from which aspirations emerge. In his book *The Capacity to Aspire*, Appadurai offered insights into how emerging countries and populations find difficulty in building a future based on their past culture. The official and mainstream discourse in China depicts a rather linear life to aspire to: study hard, work hard, have a family, and contribute to a harmonious and collective society. Since 2013, to the slogan of "Chinese dream" the slogan of "the new normal" has been added to counterbalance the slowing down of the economy.[2] In 2021, the slogan of "common prosperity" reemerged from the 1950s, giving impulse to the country's aim to become an advanced modern economy by 2050. This is the economic and social environment the post-1990s youth are facing, which offers the values of work, life, and consumption to abide by.

Chinese economic growth contributes to building youth confidence and aspirations for the future. In terms of fashion creative output, Mainland China is in the process of cultivating designer brands to be exported internationally in the mid- to long-term, after strengthening their foothold in their domestic market. In this context, it is significant

[1] Fashion studies are a new area of study that uses multiple disciplines to examine fashion through the lens of sociology, history, the arts, etc. Fashionology studies the social production processes related to fashion. Clothing items become fashion items through a process of transformation and their relationship to specific institutions (Kawamura, 2018).

[2] The concept of Chinese dream was introduced by the President in 2012, and it serves to give a common goal to increase nationalism. The term "new normal" refers to a slower economic growth rate in the last 15 years that has required a rebalancing toward a consumption-driven economy, after an investment-led economy.

to understand the evolution of China's most active and promising demographic group, Gen Z born after 1997 (Dimock, 2019), the next leading cohort of entrepreneurs, creators, and consumers. Yet, as the number of educated youths increases and as they are exposed to information within local limits, as well as value systems and alternative lifestyles from the world, some diverge from the ideal ideology. This may explain the recent controls from media and government bodies.

The dreams and struggles of the young generations are examined by Chinese sociologists. They study youths' vision of the world, including their use of digital technologies, as this generation will shape the future of a country that aims to become a world leader (Li, 2021). Li Chunling (2021) showed that millennials are differentiated in terms of gender, geographic origin, and their status as urban and rural, and examines their position in a rich China. Gen Z in China has 170 million members and combined with 350 million millennials, they represent more than half the population of Europe.

Additionally, in the last decade, technology has increased the phenomenon of interconnectedness among all players, connecting local and global markets with a heightened efficiency and speed. Thanks to a highly digitized world, the daily life and thoughts of these young generations are visible, both by marketers and governments, when compared with past generations. Their lifestyle, their interests, their behavior, and their identities will have an impact on social trends, the fashion business, and the future. "As in the West, they (Chinese Gen Z) are digital native beings who don't waste much time on making distinctions between real and virtual life," stated Vogue Business in China (2021), based on a survey of 8,000 Chinese members of Gen Z.

The Gen Z segment represents 30% of consumption in the country. Born between the late 1990s and early 2010s, they represent about 15% of the population (McKinsey, 2020a, 2020b). Their spending power and aspirations may set the pace for the global fashion and luxury markets. In other words, fashion echoes the mechanisms of other creative industries, placing talent, imagination, and creativity at its core (UNESCO, 2013). Using the lens of fashion to study young people, as creators and consumers, is in line with a creative industry that stands at the crossroads of art, industry, and culture (Blaszczyk, 2008), even though it is not part of the core of the concentric model of creative and cultural industries (CCIs) model developed by Throsby (2008).

The myth of Shanghai city is based on a period of cultural and economic growth that took place in the early 1900s. The myth still influences perceptions of the city today, and the city itself plays a role in shaping today's Chinese fashion, in terms of consumption and creation. The young Chinese designers, artists, and photographers I interviewed in the last decade often graduated from design schools located in fashion capitals like New York or London, to complement their curriculum. Most expressed their decision to be based in Shanghai city on their return, to benefit from its unique ecosystem, even if they originated from other provinces in China. Shanghai is characterized by a combination of elements that help creatives to work. The city's urban infrastructure and its productive capacity combine a variety of fashion and art venues with a consumer appetite for newness and exploration, established distribution networks, media organizations and experts, a strong business mindset, the city's unique international flair, and a mythical past.

The concept of CCIs became central to national economies in the last three decades. In the United Kingdom, under the government of Tony Blair in 1998, the Ministry of Digital, Media, Culture, and Sports issued the Creative Industries Mapping Documents report. It triggered several countries to list the industries considered to be "creative." The report acknowledged the shift toward innovation and knowledge-driven economies, the status of enterprises, and role of the creative people employed, increasing support from the government as a result (UNESCO, 2013). According to the UNESCO report on the Creative Economy, first published in 2008, fashion is one of these industries.

Throsby (2008) created a theoretical framework to categorize the CCIs in concentric circles. The arts are located at the center, and fashion is considered part of the related industries in the outer circles. When applying these frameworks to China, we need to examine the relation between culture and fashion as well. The cultural development of China is gaining momentum both domestically and abroad for geopolitical reasons as well. Wu (2018) argued that cultural soft power plays a role in national branding, image construction, and in the influence of China internationally. However, Keane (2016) suggested that Chinese practitioners, producers, and investors lack an understanding of global markets and audiences. This may stem from the high intervention of the government in the Chinese cultural output. These interventions raise questions about what constitutes the core of China's culture today, and the creation of Chinese fashion, as a related industry, following Throsby's framework. By considering growing urbanization, coupled with an increasing use of technology, this study joins these two angles using the concept of ***phygitalization***[3] as a framework to study fashion in a social context: (1) physical, (2) digital-virtual, and (3) socio-cultural. First, by ***physical*** we mean the city as a place where fashion creation and consumption are rooted, embodied, and exposed. This dimension reflects the role of the creative economy at the city scale, and the policies put in place to support CCIs such as fashion. Secondly, some disruptions caused by ***digital*** advances in the diffusion and consumption of fashion are examined. Thirdly, we position the physical and digital-virtual worlds in the context of ***sociocultural*** trends in China.

## 3 Fashion Is Embedded in the Physical World

The study of place and space is interdisciplinary, using concepts from geography, urban studies, history, architecture, and sociology. Lefebvre and Nicholson-Smith (1991) and Soja (2000) argued that space has physical and social dimensions imbued with meaning that stems from social practices. Potvin (2009) underlined that literature on fashion, place, and space focuses mainly on capitalistic consumer culture, rather than on social relationships and cultural practices. He demonstrated the intricate connections between the subjective and objective dimensions in the display and representation of fashion in various cities over two centuries. This approach is instrumental to examining the city of Shanghai as a fashion capital, in its subjective and objective dimensions, that add symbolic value to its creative industries.

Space is difficult to define; it is generic and carries no meaning per se. Place, however, is embedded in a context that carries both meaning and value, and it is defined through tangible and intangible elements. Hence the phygital world intertwines spaces and places and questions the role of culture hereafter. In fashion capitals, architects and fashion designers can create and present their work in both physical and virtual spaces and contribute to forging a city 's identity.

[3] Phygital is understood as a system of interaction in the new world when digital space penetrates the physical and integrates with a person. In marketing it describes blending physical and digital experiences.

In this chapter, I argue that the move of distribution and consumption online and the use of VR (virtual reality) communication do not necessarily weaken the importance of the physical spaces in cities. They add immersive dimensions to events and runways. Fashion is still tied to physical places where social and cultural practices develop. These physical places include design studios, art and creative clusters, design fairs, and tradeshows on the one hand, where professionals gather. On the other hand, users socialize with each other and their communities in physical spaces such as art museums, fashion venues, shopping streets, cultural events, and informal happenings. Creators and consumers are connected phygitally.

Moreover, this empirical research on the unique sensibilities of Gen Z with relation to technology leads us to suggest that the Chinese Gen Z has the ability to disrupt these long-standing relations and cultural practices. Being both involved in creation and consumption, they are able to invent new dimensions beyond traditional business models, previously unheard of. Since the pandemic in 2020, the acceleration of the use of 3D technologies has pushed the whole fashion value chain into the virtual world, from design and patternmaking to merchandising to digitalized sampling and fashion shows, and distribution.

### *The History of Shanghai and Fashion*

Shanghai fashion finds its roots in a long industrial history, merging local and global influences, including cultural and technological transfers. Developing local craftsmanship and tailoring knowhow since the mid-nineteenth century, Shanghai bears a significant role in the Chinese fashion industry to the present day. Shanghai's cultural diversity and openness stems from more than a century of economic and cultural exchange with the world, as a harbor city on the Yangtze River. Shanghai's residents have absorbed and created many trends, and the city was the cradle of the Chinese creative industries in the early twentieth century.

Until the second Sino-Japanese War (1937–1945), a Shanghai style was developing, called *haipai*. Initially used negatively by Beijing intellectuals to describe a western-oriented city, in contrast with the capital city, the term became a positive way to encompass the creative output of Shanghai. According to Pan's (2008, 2009) description of the heyday of Shanghai from the 1920s to the 1940s, no place was more modern than Shanghai, with its mix of Chinese aesthetics, western influences, art, and culture, all blended together in a unique local *haipai* style. Underground artists, designers, architects, patrons, and politicians created a singular portrait and narrative of a city that has lasted until now, when Shanghai entered a new creative age. Lindgren (2013), who examined the uniqueness of Chinese fashion designers, argued that Shanghai has a specific historical legacy to build upon. The myth of Shanghai from that time fuels the city narrative of "Made in Shanghai" brands, from fashion to cosmetics. The Bund area, along the Huangpu River, is characterized by colonial heritage buildings, and is part of its 'multi-layered history.' After a dark period from 1949 to early 1980s, the city transformed from a trading district to a cityscape devoted to finance and leisure (Henriot, 2010).

After decades of turmoil, an ecosystem based on industrial development and privatization emerged starting in the early 1980s. China became the leading world producer of clothing. In the following decade, the manufacturing industry transitioned into what we call today a 'knowledge-driven economy' that connects a network of talented start-ups, multinationals, and overseas Chinese investors through digitization. From the late 1990s to the early 2000s, the country's burgeoning consumer society became the target of established and international brands. China rapidly moved up the value chain and these changes culminated in the mobile commerce revolution we are witnessing today. Shanghai steadily transformed into a city of consumption, attracting business players from near and afar. In 1992, the central government in China took measures to relaunch Shanghai as a business city.

Shanghai's potential as an influential and creative city has grown steadily (Keane, 2013). FDI (foreign direct investment) from global business networks and from a long-term national policy supported this growth. In February 2010, Shanghai joined UNESCO's creative cities network, the same year it hosted the World Expo. Around the time of the Expo, infrastructure, new economic policies, and a massive long-term urbanization plan led to a rapid expansion unheard of in the West. New consumer demand and a buoyant economy attracted foreign designers and architects in charge of creating attractive world-class venues[4] and building the identity of a modern global city.

[4] Interview with Mrs. Margaux Lhermitte, Interior Designer, former GM of Naço Architectures Agency in Shanghai, Shanghai, 2018.

Since the 2010s, Shanghai's soft power has expanded, and it is fueling the fashion market's attractiveness. Since the Expo, Shanghai has increasingly invested in its art scene in a more systematic way. Public and private institutions opened world-class museums and galleries, organized design fairs and art exhibitions, and sealed multiple international partnerships. For instance, the French Pompidou Museum opened in 2019, in collaboration with the West Bund Development Group, for a period of five years (Pompidou Center). These developments raise a question: is Shanghai on the verge of becoming a creative hub?[5] (British Council, 2016). The pulse of Shanghai's development is even more complex since the COVID-19 pandemic, which resulted in closing the borders to outsiders and returning the country to some of its previous physical isolation from the rest of the world.

### *Urbanization and Fashion in Shanghai*

Scanning fashion cities and consumers with a designer's mindset was instrumental in my investigation of Shanghai, where future trends crystallize in front of our eyes in places, and in the virtual world in spaces. Designers instinctively implement applied research by anticipating future trends based on the smallest signs of change in society, be it a counterculture, the innovative usage of a product, the detail of a cloth, the shape of an art piece, or blog content. The current sprawling urbanization in China sets the scene for increased creation, production, and consumption, although this system needs to be reconsidered in light of its negative environmental and social impact. The changing landscape of mega-cities gives birth to social transformations that modify the distribution of economic power, education, family traditions, and consumption.

Fashion consumption grows with demographic and economic transformations led by the Chinese middle class, which will soon represent the equivalent of several countries (McKinsey, 2021). At the world level, in 1950, 30% of the country's population was urban. As of 2018, 55% lived in urban areas. By 2050, it is projected that this figure will reach 68% (UN, 2018). China follows this world trend. Sixteen cities besides Shanghai (24 million) gather more than ten million inhabitants, such as

[5] The British Council defines creative hubs as physical and digital spaces that attract people from a range of backgrounds with a focus on developing digital technology, enterprise and social innovation. These hubs facilitate collaborations.

Chongqing (31 million), Beijing (21 million), and Chengdu (16 million). Chinese cities attract rural citizens and increase a social divide. They also create a new population mix and modify individual if not national identities.

Breward and Gilbert (2006) compared fashion world cities and the relationship between metropolitan modernity and fashion culture. More specifically, they highlight the status of fashion capitals as part of the cultural economy. The municipality of Shanghai aspires to position itself as one of China's fashion cities, but it faces multiple challenges as the "Made in China" label still suffers from low esteem in the world's view, regardless of the actual quality of products. Let us have a glimpse at Shanghai's history to understand its uniqueness and the legitimacy of its aim to become a global and creative fashion city.

### *The Myth of Shanghai Is Still Attractive to Today's Youth*

Fashion is located in space; it emanates from a culture, a country, and often a city (Potvin, 2009). The historical and cultural background of the city is a source of narratives that increase its mythology, as well as the impact of the brands created there. The narrative around the mythical fashion city of the first quarter of the twentieth century is still alive today. Although a century separates the heyday of Shanghai's creative era from today's modern city, observers and visitors can feel its heritage while also feeling the pulse of a global hub in the making. Some heritage buildings have been renovated in their original form or recreated. Some districts aim to enhance their grounded urban identity, either old or newly recreated in the past style, as in Xintiandi or Jing'an area. These sites attract visitors from several generations, as well as visitors from out of town.

A visit to the Shanghai-based foundation of the Italian brand Prada, on its opening day in 2017, is engraved in my memory. The foundation is located in a historical building dating from 1918, on the corner of Nanjing Road, which was meticulously renovated by Chinese and Italian craftsmen. I was able to witness the pride of the local Shanghainese for their city's history. Most of the visitors were not fans of the Italian brand, as one might have expected; rather, among the audience were 80-year-old citizens who wanted to discover the interior of a house that used to belong to one of the country's wealthiest families, the Rong Zhai, during their youth. Proudly posing in the art deco central living room, these elegant and humble women, dressed in simple attire, were taking selfies on their smartphones, to share with their friends or followers.

Likewise, young people flock from the suburban areas to experience Shanghai's increasing modernity, as well as to admire renovated heritage buildings. They target shopping districts on weekends, and increasingly cultural sites, old and new. For instance, on Huai Hai Road, Gen Z cohorts gathered every weekend after the end of the confinement in 2020 in a craze to take selfies in emblematic locations and art deco settings, or to discover architects that built the cachet of this city. For example, Hungarian architect László Hudec was an important figure in Shanghai in the 1920–1940s. Visitors can still see his architecture in large buildings, hotels, banks, schools, and cinemas, to this day. He contributed to the Shanghai style of culture and spirit. The contrast between old and new districts juxtaposed, and old and young generations in search of unique and authentic experiences, give a sense of being witness to a transformation. Older generations buy classic music records in a vintage shop, driven by nostalgia from their youth and western-style dance halls, while today's youth take selfies of their Italian ice cream next door, giving different and complex meanings to urban culture.[6] Gen Z rejuvenates the city's myth in their own way, and with their techno-driven communication styles.

The policies of spatial development in Shanghai have influenced society, mainly through the creation of commercial areas for economic reasons. The sophisticated Xintiandi district, the Huai Hai Road and IAPM mall, the iconic shopping street of Nanjing Road, Taikoo Hui shopping center, Global Harbor, Lujiazui district IFC, and Shanghai Tower are just examples of the real estate investment that is transforming the city landscape alongside people's habits. As a result, young people gather for a shopping frenzy on weekends, despite the accessibility of e-commerce and m-commerce (on their smartphones). China represented almost 50% of global e-commerce before COVID-19 (McKinsey, 2020a, 2020b). What makes youth still want to gather physically?

A physical presence is part of phygital strategies, including experiential marketing, which are transforming the retail experience into a leisurely activity that creates fun memories that leads to diffusing pictures taken in meaningful locations, making it worth the trip in person. The new art districts of downtown West Bund are also creating a reason for

[6] Interview with a classic music shop owner, Huai Hai Road, 2020.

young people to leave the comfort of their homes, and to expose themselves to contemporary art, lavishly renovated riverbanks, and luxurious surroundings.

On the other hand, some young people are on a quest for community connection with like-minded people. Eco-conscious urban youth explore the organic markets in downtown alleys or venture out into suburban farms on Chongming Island. If Shanghai is considered a microcosm or prototype of the future from the standpoint of provincial Chinese towns, one can expect replicas of the Shanghai lifestyle and trends in other parts of the country. Considering the size of each Chinese province, comparable to a European country, foreign players ought to follow and anticipate new business developments, disruptive consumer attitudes, product inventions, and sociocultural evolutions originating throughout the country.

## 4 New Tech Paths for Fashion in China

In March 2021, China's National People's Congress (NPC) outlined the country's 14th Five-Year Plan, covering the period 2021–2025. The goal for the digital economy's share of the GDP is set at 10% in 2025, compared to 7.8% in 2020. Technology lies at the heart of the plan, and the innovation ecosystem needs to be reinforced through collaborations and intellectual property protection (Kaja et al., 2021). Spanning the government's long-term vision with the short cycle of daily consumption of a billion inhabitants, technological advances set the pace.

Although apparel production is not prominent anymore in the industrial development of China, the country's entry into WTO in 2001 has accelerated the mechanisms to transform the ecosystem, facing aggressive high fashion foreign players entering the market. Moreover, fashion plays a new role in society as a visible consumer good that requires constant innovative input. Innovation is embedded in a social system that can increase or slow down its diffusion (Rogers, 2003). Fashion can both absorb social trends and influence society in return.

The fashion market in China has grown steadily with the greater purchasing power of the population since the 2000s. Foreign entrants have increased the competition targeting the burgeoning consumer society. As the population increased its level of education and exposure to fashion media through the Internet, the market became increasingly challenging. Millions of consumers shifted away from functional clothing to select more fashionable styles that reflected their quest for enhanced identity and modernity in major cities.

Technology and innovation are present all along the value chain[7] of the fashion world, from consumer analysis to sales forecasting, from smart material[8] to the creative processes to develop products, from logistics to communication. Digital platforms, e-commerce, and social media have revolutionized the fashion industry and greatly accelerated a process that used to take months to diffuse products and concepts to the end-user. Benetton from Italy was one of the leaders of to revolutionize the supply chain, connecting stores to their factories. Then the logistics systems continued to be reinvented by Zara from Spain and were widened to Chinese apparel players like Bosideng or Metersbonwe that operate across countries and have omnichannel strategies. In 2018, Alibaba group launched its first AI concept store, to simplify the customers' shopping experience (Magana, 2018). These stores combine intelligent garment tags, collect information on customers, and bridge the gap between physical and digital retail stores. The two systems are merging and blurring, creating a new paradigm (Duhan & Singh, 2019).

One example of the blurring between physical and digital shopping experiences is the local fast-fashion brand, Urban Revivo. The brand was launched in 2006 in Guangzhou province, and it opened abroad in Singapore in 2017 for the first time. In 2018, they renovated an outstanding location on Huai Hai road of 1500 square meters. Since 2019, in their store located in the River Mall shopping center of Pudong district in Shanghai, virtual fitting rooms enable body measurements with sensors and cameras, and store customers' data. Scanning a QR code, they can see how they would look like, and get product suggestions (Archdaily.com, 2018). Their store is equipped with vocal recognition from the entrance.

The emergence of the Internet has created opportunities, as well as challenges for fashion producers and retailers who are not able to combine

[7] In the fashion business, the value chain starts with the choice of material used to make the final product. The next steps in the chain consist of production, distribution and retail until the item reaches the end users.

[8] Smart materials can be called intelligent materials. They are designed to have specific properties in reaction to the environment. They can adapt to the body temperature, and to external stimuli such as moisture, light and electric fields. They are incorporated in a wide range of products for their level of functionality, and the use of energy and communication technology. They can be used in fashion and other industries. The Chinese government is investing heavily in this research.

offline with online retailing strategies. Technology enables omnichannel distribution and 360° media campaigns. AI is the next challenge to capture consumers' profiles and aspirations.

### *Targeting Chinese Consumers Through Technology*

In the last 15 years, traditional fashion retailers had to transition from multichannel to omnichannel[9] strategies (Bèzes, 2018). Sharing data about customers across channels can effectively increase sales during the decision-making process, which spans customers' search for information, to the selection process, to purchasing items. Deloitte's report (2018) highlighted that the ultimate challenge of the fashion industry will be its digital transformation throughout its entire organizational structure. The availability of big data and analytics to analyze the market and the consumers will allow players to navigate this complex environment.

Chinese fashion players are now equipped with an array of data and digital tools that have allowed them to leapfrog the technological revolution faster than long-established companies in mature countries. In the fashion business, agility is a key driver of success (McKinsey and Business of Fashion, 2020). In the last decade, Chinese companies have grown stronger at targeting local consumers, developing a deeper understanding of the Chinese consumers' aspirations than foreign players. Technology accelerated the speed of change, the geographic reach, and the spread of information. It has stimulated the market growth with platforms, quick payment methods, and local influencers.[10] The boundaries are blurred between online and offline distribution, and between distribution and communication activities as well. Big data, demand sensing, social buzz, and consumer profiles are gathered in digital platforms to forecast and optimize the fashion value chain. In this process, fashion forecasting usually helps manufacturers anticipate digital and other trends.

Fashion forecasting is a service and method commonly used by the fashion industry in mature economies to foresee market trends, tap into consumer aspirations, and map technological advances to integrate into

[9] Omnichannel refers to distributing to multiple channels, whether in physical stores, online platforms, and mobile phones, thus providing the consumer with a uniform and seamless shopping experience.

[10] Interview with Mr. Xavier Brochart, Consultant in Digital Marketing, November 2021.

the production and marketing of textiles and fashion items. These service companies provide ideas and consulting to manufacturers and buyers for the upcoming seasons based on the analysis of data on market trends, consumers, and offerings in the distribution chain. Forecasting companies can access trends instantaneously among their professional clients, accelerating the whole fashion lifecycle. For instance, photo sharing through digital devices and software from one part of the world to the other has spread trends faster (Kim et al., 2021).

In China, the speed of changes in the market does not allow for long-term anticipation of consumer aspirations, even with forecasting models. Fashion forecasting in China is replaced by instantaneous data analysis available to professionals. They geolocalize users, gather real-time trending items, preferences, payment data, in stores and online, and connect them to factories' facilities. As a result, the long-standing forecasting industry from mature fashion countries is not able to compete with the speed of information in China, nor with local needs.

### *Immersive Fashion Brands, Culture, and the Metaverse*

Technological inventions rapidly contribute to creating an immersive experience with fashion brands. On the one hand, the O2O (online to offline) commerce and the *phygitalization* of marketing have opened new paths in the last few years. They also compete in the minds of consumers at the level of experience and unforgettable memories in the mind of consumers. Marketing decisions are increasingly data-driven, and consumers' behaviors are tracked, to infer on their preferences, and to personalize interactions. More recently the fashion industry is considering how to use metaverse technology. It will only increase the merging of physical and virtual worlds (van der Merwe, 2021). The metaverse market is deemed to reach 800 billion dollars by 2024 (Bloomberg Intelligence, 2021). GenZ and digital natives are particularly open to such disruptions. Oh and Nah (2022) argued that the digital generation is influenced by fashion influencers, and technology allows for the expression of individual values and emotional details, more than trends. The cultural context has an impact on the consumer and needs to be considered. Nam and Kannan (2020) highlight those offline and online touchpoints are likely to be more integrated along the customer journey in collectivist cultures like China.

Imported fashion and luxury brands set the pace of the market in terms of cultural experiences that blend physical and digital technologies, whether in stores or in art exhibitions. They understand the appeal of technology among Chinese young generations. The Italian brand Valentino created an immersive exhibition in November 2021, "Re-Signify Part One Shanghai" in the Power Station of Art Museum, presenting elements of the brand, in a non-chronological manner. They used phygital and multimedia display of fashion items, photographs, videos, and cinema surrounding the visitors. It meant to connect the dots for multiple generations of consumers, combining digital and physical elements, launching campaigns that are cultural, and not just commercial. They aim to appeal to the emerging Chinese cultural consumer by blending technology with culture, in a market led by large e-commerce platforms like Tencent, Tmall, and Baidu groups.

Content marketing is at the heart of digital campaigns. Compared to the West, Chinese consumers need more information on brands; "they need three to five times more information," even on a simple product, argues Mr. Brochart, an expert in digital marketing in China. He also underlines that the Chinese writing system makes it possible to condense a much larger amount of data on the screen of a smartphone when compared to Roman letters. Consequently, young consumers are very informed and knowledgeable. In a country known for a highly competitive school system, it is important to demonstrate knowledge to one's peers, even on brands.[11]

Livestreaming is the most rapidly evolving communication tool in China. Nowadays fashion and beauty companies consider that livestreaming can engage their Chinese customers and communities and generate rapid sales revenue. It has advantages and pitfalls, such as the Chinese stars that complained about L'Oréal's misleading discounts during the November singles' day shopping festival (People's Daily Online, 2021).

[11] Interview with Mr. Xavier Brochart, Digital marketing consultant who worked in China for 14 years, November 17th, 2021.

The metaverse[12] is the next world being explored by fashion companies, and if the West is still doubtful on its benefits and risks, young Chinese consumers are likely to engage quickly in this virtual world. This attraction to technology is comparable to other east Asian countries like Singapore, Japan, and South Korea. However, fashion players need to consider that educated Gen Z cohorts have started to demonstrate a more developed sense of privacy, and that they are likely to fear digital counterfeit on the metaverse, warns a strategic planner in luxury communication in Shanghai.[13] Technology also allows consumers to turn down brands on social media, on the base of counterfeit and plagiarism, such as the case of the Chinese high street apparel brand Peacebird in 2021.

### *Chinese Brands and Fashion Designers*

The transformation of "clothing" into "fashion" is a process, a sociological phenomenon embedded in a symbolic value system and culture (Craik, 2003; Kawamura, 2004). Much like other countries, there are different kinds of fashion players in mainland China. Brands launched by Chinese apparel makers need to be distinguished from those created by fashion designers. They differ in terms of design originality, their company size, their financial backup, and their business model. Large Chinese apparel makers, such as Bosideng, Urban Revivo, Peacebird, Ochirly, Me & City, manage hundreds of shops, and they have the means to invest heavily in digital media for their reputation abroad. They can be compared to apparel giants like Gap (USA), H&M (Sweden), Uniqlo (Japan), and Zara (Spain). However, the focus here is on Chinese fashion designers because they create original ideas eligible to be protected by intellectual property rights, as defined by official reports and theorists on CCIs, like Howkins (2001); these designers aim to express strong aesthetics and cultural identities. As such, some are displayed in art museums.

Networks of creation, production, distribution, and consumption are much studied in western fashion markets, but little is known of the

[12] The term "metaverse" was coined in 1992 by novelist Neal Stephenson. Currently it refers to an immersive virtual world, computer generated, where people can gather, work, and will be able to buy. In October 2021, Facebook founder Zuckerberg announced that his company will be called Meta.

[13] Interview with Mrs. Jade Camus, Strategic Planner, Adventi PR Agency in Shanghai, November 21st, 2021.

Chinese equivalent. Art exhibitions dedicated to fashion designers are increasing in Shanghai, and some feature Chinese-born designers like Anna Sui. I had the chance to visit Anna Sui's exhibition in 2020. What was striking was how the curators, who were from the UK, decisively highlighted the relation between her fashion and youth music in New York City. The exhibit clearly presented Anna Sui's sources of inspiration in the street culture, the bands, and the artistic movements of that time. She was part of a group of young artists who captured the vibe of the time and the place and combined them with her own creative skills. However, in the context of Mainland China, this phenomenon is currently hardly visible or perhaps not even possible, for reasons beyond pandemic-related safety measures. Youth gatherings are controlled and not encouraged, unless they are consumption driven. Is this the ultimate space of expression?

Defining Chinese fashion as being designed in Mainland China, or by designers of Chinese origin wherever they live, could be the subject of debate. Anna Sui, mentioned earlier, Vivienne Tam, Jimmy Choo, Philip Lim, Jason Wu, and Alexander Wang have paved the way for Asian designers in the American market, after the boom of Japanese-born designers. Lindgren (2013) distinguished Chinese designers that have entered the global fashion system from those that are based locally, that lack a cultural bedrock such as what exists in other fashion environments. He revealed that some designers are exploring a distinct Chinese aesthetic, away from what western viewers deem as representing Chinese creativity. My field research and interviews confirm Lindgren's observations; however, I question if the young generations can identify with the Chinese aesthetics offered by these designers. I also wonder if the world will be able to accept them to the way they accepted the wave of Japanese designers who shook the world of fashion in the 1980–1990s (Chrétien-Ichikawa, 2012).

China is set to emerge in the creative world. Young people are questioning their role and position among the world's creators and leading economies. Some have witnessed foreign creativity. Western creativity is based on disruption, whereas Chinese creativity is more harmonious and incremental (Keane & Jing Zhao, 2014). As in other countries, Chinese designers are influenced by their generation, and they influence it in return, and some experienced disruption abroad. As a matter of fact, Christine Tsui is exploring this path. One of the first to analyze Chinese fashion, she interviewed designers born between the 1960s and 1980s for her pioneer book *China Fashion* (2013a). In 2017, she noticed a generational shift in Shanghai Fashion Week. She interviewed some post-1990s fashion designers to understand their vision, such as Mukzin. She found that what distinguishes them is precisely their experience abroad, graduating from Central Saint Martins in London, or Parsons School of Design in New York, for instance. This generation is characterized by "a spirit of revolt and subversion" (Tsui, 2017) and the influence of Internet, the West, and abundance. Compared to their elders, they are more conscious of societal issues, world events, gender values, and inequality. Consequently, their designs blur cultures and gender and make stronger statements, caring less about judgments. They also reflect the attitude of customers of the same generation. Tsui (2017) said, "The combination of brave designers and the brave customers inspires a diverse fashion world for the young."

Young Chinese designers find new paths to diffuse their work. Some don't bother to find retail spaces, and they are able to sell on WeChat accounts or specialized platforms to their small community of followers and fans.[14] Thanks to the technology of the last few years, an invisible virtual world of fashion creation has developed parallel to the traditional prime locations and shopping malls, where previous generations used to shop. Digital devices have encouraged a whole generation to dialogue directly with their consumer base, much like the first age of fashion houses, at a time when there were few intermediaries.

## 5 Fashion Echoes the Sociocultural Transformations of China

After having examined some aspects of the physical and digital evolution of fashion in Shanghai, the broader sociocultural context provides keys to understanding the specificities of Chinese youth. Historian Paul Clark (2012) observed that Chinese youth asserted their identity during the 1960–1970s Cultural Revolution, and it is not until the late 1980s that they started to be influenced by music and sports. The Internet brought information from the world and provided a new space for expression. Their aspirations have transformed into a youth culture with local roots

[14] Interview with Mrs. Lu Ming, Fashion Designer, Shanghai, 2020.

and international elements because of the media. The post-1990s generation (*hulian wang yuan zhumin*) was particularly affected by the digital revolution (Li, 2021a). Empirical research, interviews, field observations, scholarly work, and recent press form the base of this fifth part.

### *Chinese Digital Natives, Global Culture, and Acculturation*

By 2025, half of all Asia Pacific consumers will be part of the millennial and Gen Z generations, representing a major economic driver, according to a survey by Kim et al. (2020) for McKinsey. Implemented across the Asian Gen Z population, the survey highlights the emergence of five social trends: the thoughtful use of social media, wanting it all, the preference for unique brands, the influence of video content, and being perceived as environmentally conscious without paying extra for it.

In the last 40 years, the outside world, the global culture, and consumerist principles have influenced Chinese youth who are open to change, unless taught otherwise. There used to be a strong divide between urban and rural populations (Liu, 2011) in terms of income and exposure to information, until infrastructure enabled social media to reach remote parts of the country. The diffusion of livestreaming videos, images, and e-commerce platforms contributes to the exposure of tens of millions of provincial users, to consumerist values present in affluent coastal regions. Consequently, today's Gen Z cohort is even more connected and demanding. In recent years, citizens of the most modern cities also demonstrate a thirst for more aesthetic design, innovativeness, and a sense of meaning beyond consumption, although still a niche trend. The youth are eager to jump on board with new trends and influencers, yet under the scrutiny of authorized media bodies.

Western values are increasingly being considered as a potential negative influence in China in the last few years. They permeate global youth culture in music, videos, cinema, and publishing, in other words, through the CCIs. The Chinese government's intention to protect Chinese youth against global soft power is political, and instrumental to building a stronger national spirit (Fish, 2017). One can perceive these policies that target the media as going against globalization, on the one hand. On the other hand, the Chinese government considers that there is a need to reinforce a national cohesion and identity. Consequently, Gen Z attitudes and sexual behaviors are not entirely approved by the central state (Chi et al., 2012). More recently, media regulators have prohibited idols of Chinese pop music that are seen as "deforming aesthetics" that influence their youth negatively. The intrusion of regulators in the daily life of Gen Z's world of entertainment and leisure may be partly explained by the theories of acculturation.[15]

Fashion trends emerge from an interplay between sociocultural factors and the evolution of consumers (Kim et al., 2021). Some trends are short-lived while others are the consequence of deep societal shifts, such as the ineluctable rise of sustainable fashion. Fashion trends can emanate from social movements, counterculture and reactions of the youth to their environment. "Counterculture refers to the values, beliefs and attitudes, that is the culture, of a minority group that is in opposition to the mainstream or ascendant culture." (Barker, 2004, p. 36). Young generations have the power to shake societies and governments, as can be seen in world history. And social media have become instrumental to questioning authority (Deloitte, 2021). China banned foreign social media providers Facebook, Twitter, Google, and WhatsApp in 2009, in order to avoid propagating unwanted and politically sensitive news. Consequently, the young generations of Chinese have limited access to world information. However, in the context of Mainland China, where freedom of speech is monitored, some youths are creative in finding ways to express their novel ideas, concepts, lifestyle, or criticism, without disturbing the mainstream consensus.

Millennial consumers, born between 1981 and 1996 (Dimock, 2019) are also under the scrutiny of fashion brands. New generations of designers emerge, answering the needs of local consumers who are increasingly in search of uniqueness. The following section will explore how companies use social media to target specific segments of the population, and to influence millions of consumers. On the one hand, digital platforms and influencers contribute to shaping nationwide consumer habits. On the other hand, marginal urban identities appear, giving signs of a creative impulse, beyond consumption.

## *Virtual Identities of the Past and Future*

One afternoon in the West Bund Area, along the Huangpu River, I attended an exhibition of Chanel in a gigantic space that could fit an

[15] Acculturation is a process that results in changes occurring when cultures come into contact.

airplane. It presented the brand's original collection of jewelry, outfits, movies, and books. In the center of the space, a white wall with a black Chanel logo set the stage for visitors to portray themselves as stars, with selfies. Outside, slender young Chinese women were taking pictures of each other. Sitting against the background of 1950s style furniture in a trendy coffee shop, these women seemed to create an image of themselves, sculpting every detail of their appearance and model-like poses. They wore "Instagram-able" clothes, shoes, makeup, and accessories—or should we say "WeChat-able"?

Within the lapse of a few years, prime locations like this one have sprung up around the city. They include trendy coffee shops, ice cream parlors, wine bars, rooftops, and artsy locations. Many have invested in their interior design in order to be the backstage for millennials and Gen Z looking for the best spot. The city is their stage. Holding a glass of wine in posh Italian restaurants, they create an imagined and perfect self, an identity that can be sent to their friends and followers, without necessarily eating the food. Their most intricate clothes and makeup have transformed them into doll-like women, and handsome men, to be portrayed on social media. Technology has influenced the social environment and people's gestures, clothing, food habits, facial expressions, and their choice of leisure, pets, and cars. Consumer goods, especially luxury brands, are displayed ferociously, as a vehicle and enhancer of their newly acquired or dreamed status. Their fashionable image is profusely shared if not created in the virtual world, through the functionalities of apps that erase pimples, add a sparkle in their eyes, and whiten their skin tone. Is this their real or ideal identity?

On the other end of the spectrum, there are Gen Z communities who search for traditional Chinese experiences, and for elements of identity within their cultural roots and their past, both more recent and remote. For their wedding pictures, couples stroll in the old districts of Shanghai or Suzhou city nearby, wearing 1920s styles, borrowed for the day. Their photographer conspicuously guides their gestures and facial expressions while they face the detail of a bridge, a half-torn picture on a brick wall, or sit on a wooden bench to immortalize their love. If the picture were in black and white, it could elicit memories of the heyday of Shanghai 100 years ago.

One day, I was teaching about luxury and heritage in a Chinese university to prepare an elite class with high credentials to pursue their studies in France at the doctoral level. While sharing the concept of transmission of family heritage through objects from one generation to another, such as of furniture, jewelry, and accessories among European families, one young woman burst into tears: “We don’t have that here, it is gone. We had to hide it, burn it, or pretend,” she said. I was touched by her reaction and explained that historical facts are beyond our understanding, but that her generation has a role to play in the rejuvenation of Chinese culture. I highlighted that a stay abroad could reinforce a sense of one’s own identity and allow to position oneself in the broader world culture.

Nostalgia for a long gone past is emerging stronger in the last ten years maybe for this reason: a lack of transmitted material heritage. The yearning for lost memories may be at the origin of the vintage craze, but it takes on a different angle in China where 1960s–1970s attire were uniforms. What period are people looking for? Which one reveals more significance to them? As a matter of fact, vintage clothing refers to different moments of history in China than western fashion does. What if vintage meant going back centuries? Intrigued by the rise of women wearing traditional clothes, I interviewed them to understand their admiration of ancient *Han* heritage and *hanfu* clothing, referring to the Han, Tang, and Song dynasties. The search of Chinese identities and their cultural roots was at their core. Ling and Segre-Reinach’s (2018) recent book on Chinese fashion explored the multiplicity of Chinese identities, in terms of sources of inspiration and expressions. The Chinese Gen Z are creating alternative identities as well, through electronic devices that portray a beautified self and environment. Their generational discourse needs to be placed in historical context, where youth culture suffers from censorship. They are in the mist of multiple influences, from Europe and the United States, from Japan and South Korea, and from overseas Chinese communities. They are also demonstrating a quest for their roots, exploring different periods of an almost vanished Chinese culture, and reviving it to a certain extent. Indeed, the diversity of past dynasties, regional cultures, and world influences create opportunities for some, and confusion for others. How about finding refuge in a virtual world, and create an avatar of oneself either in *hanfu* or in futuristic attire?

Demna Gvasaglia, who joined Balenciaga fashion brand (Kering Group) in 2015 as art director, reflected on what is real and virtual in a world where technology dominates. The Spring 2022 collection released in June 2021 was called “Clones.” The video showed an audience sitting on both sides of a classic runway. They all wore long black clothes and held a mobile phone to take pictures in a robot-like manner, but they were not actually present. The message shown before the video went as follows: "We see our world through a filter, perfected, polished, conformed, photoshopped. We no longer decipher between unedited and altered, genuine and counterfeit, tangible and conceptual, fact and fiction, fake and deepfake. Technology creates alternative realities and identities, a world of digital clones."[16] This recent statement from a world-level fashion designer echoes what can be observed among the global youth culture, and maybe more vividly in China's comparatively recent urban culture.

How receptive are post-1990s Chinese generations to these forms of technology? A large number of Internet users have made China a profitable marketplace for fashion players. Convenience and ease of use are significant reasons for buying on the Internet, as well as saving time and money, the influence of friends and the innovativeness of Internet offerings (Wei et al., 2018). In other words, the level of acceptance of technology is one reason why online business has grown exponentially. Since 2009, the Singles' Day online shopping that takes place on November 11th has grown steadily. But an anti-consumerist group urged people to be more mindful; as a consequence, 2021 sales of 540.3 billion yuan (US$84.4 billion) grew at its slowest rate since Alibaba created this shopping extravaganza.

Furthermore, there is a rise of interest for domestically designed and produced items, or *guochao* (国潮). This term means Chinese wave, and it refers to a search for Chinese brands among generations born after the 1980–1990s, such as the sportswear brand Li-Ning, gaining popularity. This trend became prominent during the past five years and Chinese style branding has provided a narrative to the national identity. This emerging phenomenon refers to the country's rejuvenation of a material culture (Wang, 2022).

In terms of purchasing behavior, the young Chinese segment has been particularly impacted by technological disruptions for several reasons. Since the country's 2001 entry into WTO, fashion items originally meant for export were made available for domestic consumption. This entailed developing brick-and-mortar retail networks and communication for local players, like Metersbonwe. Brands decided to connect their factories

[16] Balenciaga unveils its 'CLONES' show Spring/Summer 2022 (2021, June 27), BALENCIAGA Clones spring 2022 digital show—Bing video.

directly with their consumers. Traditional paper magazines were also replaced by digitalized platforms, diffusing fashion trends rapidly to tens of millions of consumers for a lower cost. Finally, apps, mini-programs, and m-commerce revolutionized the whole industry (Duhan & Singh, 2019). These changes happened in a shorter span of time and on a larger scale than in Europe or the USA. And if digital technologies and media changed the environment of consumers, the usage and the nature of customer journeys differ from one country to another, depending on cultural and socioeconomic factors, and a collectivist society (Nam & Kannan, 2020). For these various cultural and technological reasons, the complexity of the fashion market has increased for foreign observers and entrants.

The gaming industry and fashion are getting closer in the last few years, with more collaborations between digital players and fashion brands to create virtual attire and accessories. Economically speaking, gaming, fashion, and consumption represent a limitless space of exploration for Chinese young urbanites from the middle class. Yet it could be argued that the outcomes of technological transformations need to be anticipated and discussed. Its social impact needs to be examined as Chinese youths are caught up between morally and politically correct content, and a search for identity. Furthermore, they are the potential prey of new digital businesses. Or can technology offer the means to create virtual worlds expressing their true aspirations, a space of identity creation and transformation?

## 6 Conclusion

This chapter examined the transformation of fashion in China through a phygital lens, and through the increasing role of the post-1990s generation. In only 40 years since the 1980s, Chinese fashion players were able to catch up with world levels of design, production, and distribution of fashion, and elaborate efficient communication campaigns, potentially reaching more than a billion inhabitants. The phygital revolution, combined with a heightened sense of culture among young consumers, is illustrated by Shanghai city; the city allows us to foresee wider changes in the years to come in other parts of the country.

First, the physical dimension of fashion was underlined, although the virtual world is gaining importance. Fashion is embedded in space, and especially in cities. From online to offline retail environments, and the development of city streets, the marketplace has evolved toward integrating relevant cultural and artistic content within marketing strategies. CCIs development can give space to young creators.

Secondly, technology enables the diffusion of ideas, concepts, and brands on the one hand. On the other hand, algorithms track the gestures of hundreds of millions of consumers' aspirations, and can even record their face, their voice, and their body shape. No other country was able to leapfrog systemic changes at such a speed and scale. No other country can either make foreign players be dependent of Gen Z reactions or boycott, within the reach of a smartphone click.

Third, 350 Chinese millennials (Daxue Consulting, 2020), and nearly 100 million Gen Z members aged 20–40, are transforming the way fashion is created and consumed within China. Concomitant to this phenomenal demographic and social change, technology added a new dimension that accelerates the mechanisms of the fashion ecosystem nationwide. In the economy of fashion, demographics are a major driver of growth and potential disruption. The growing urban young tech-savvy Gen Z cohorts, more than the previous millennials, have evolved in terms of sophistication. Even if they represent a smaller percentage, they are leading social change and consumption. If millions are thirsty for more aesthetics, meaning, and services in their lifestyle, enterprises need to adapt swiftly, whether large or small, local, or global. They do not know a world without technology at their fingertip. Both creators and urban consumers of fashion from this generation have used platforms to learn, communicate, consume, and relax. China's rapid economic development allows the revival of Chinese culture, with CCI-driven policies, young people's ideas, and technological advances. Ideas, idols, and products cross the territory at a lightning speed, diffusing a common mass culture, but also allowing high culture and niche trends to appear. Finally, this chapter contributes to the book's core focus at the crossroads of digitization, creativity, and identity. By recalling the speed of fashion development locally, and the power of digitization as a vehicle for diffusion globally, we wonder when China mainland youth fashion will reach other shores.

## References


Appadurai, A. (2004). The capacity to aspire: Culture and the terms of recognition. *Culture and Public Action, 59*, 62–63.

Archdaily.com. (2018, September 23). *UR Shanghai flagship store/DOMANI*. https://www.archdaily.com/902199/ur-shanghai-flagship-store-domani

Barker, C. (2004). *The Sage dictionary of cultural studies*. Sage.

Bèzes, C. (2018). What kind of in-store smart retailing for an omnichannel real-life experience? *Recherches et Applications en Marketing, 34*(1), 91–112.

Blaszczyk, R. L. (2008). *Producing fashion: Commerce, culture, and consumers*. University of Pennsylvania Press.

Bloomberg Intelligence. (2001). *Metaverse may be $800 billion market, next tech platform*. December 1st 2021. https://www.bloomberg.com/professional/blog/metaverse-may-be-800-billion-market-next-tech-platform/

Breward, C., & Gilbert, D. (2006). *Fashion's world cities* (Cultures of Consumption Series). Berg.

British Council. (2016). *The creative hubs report*. https://www.britishcouncil.ro/sites/default/files/creative_hubkit_en.pdf

Chi, X., Yu, L., & Winter, S. (2012). Prevalence and correlates of sexual behaviors among university students: A study in Hefei, China. *BMC Public Health, 12*(1), 1–10.

Chrétien-Ichikawa, S. (2012). *Le rôle du Japon dans la réémergence de la mode chinoise* (*The role of China in the re-emergence of Chinese fashion*) (unpublished PhD dissertation, EHESS).

Chrétien-Ichikawa, S. (2015). Shanghai, a creative fashion system under construction. *China Perspectives, 3*, 33–41.

Clark, P. (2012). *Youth culture in China: From Red Guards to netizens*. Cambridge University Press.

Craik, J. (2003). *The face of fashion: Cultural studies in fashion*. Routledge.

Daxue Consulting. (2020, June 29). *Chinese millennials' spending Behavior: Online vs. offline, domestic vs. foreign, premium vs. convenience*. Daxueconsulting.com.

Deloitte. (2018). *Global powers of luxury goods 2018*. https://www2.deloitte.com/content/dam/Deloitte/at/Documents/consumer-business/deloitte-global-powers-of-luxurygoods-2018.pdf

Deloitte. (2021). *A call for accountability and action: The Deloitte global 2021 millennial and Gen Z survey*. Deloitte.com.

Dimock, M. (2019). Defining generations: Where millennials end and Generation Z begins. *Pew Research Center*. Where Millennials end and Generation Z begins | Pew Research Center.

Duhan, P., & Singh, A. (2019). *M-Commerce, experiencing the phygital retail*. Apple Academic Press.

Finnane, A. (2008). *Changing clothes in China: Fashion, history, nation*. Columbia University Press.

Fish, E. (2017). *Why's Beijing so worried about western values infesting Chinese youth*. Chinafile.com. https://www.chinafile.com/features/whys-beijing-so-worried-about-western-values-infecting-chinas-youth

Henriot, C. (2010). The Shanghai Bund in myth and history: An essay through textual and visual sources. *Journal of Modern Chinese History, 4*(1), 1–27.

Howkins, J. (2001). *The creative economy: How people make money from ideas*. Allen Lane.

Kaja, A., Stein, S., & Xiang, T. (2021). *China's 14th Five-Year Plan (2021–2025): Signposts for doing business in China*. Global Watch Policy. https://www.globalpolicywatch.com/2021/04/chinas-14th-five-year-plan-2021-2025-signposts-for-doing-business-in-china/

Kawamura, Y. (2004). *The Japanese revolution in Paris fashion*. Berg.

Kawamura, Y. (2018). *Fashion-ology: An introduction to fashion studies* (2nd ed.). Bloomsbury.

Keane, M. (2013). *Creative industries in China: Art, design and media*. Polity.

Keane, M. (2016). Going global or going nowhere? Chinese media in a time of flux. *Media International Australia, 159*(1), 13–21.

Keane, M., & Jing Zhao, E. (2014). The reform of the cultural system: Culture, creativity and innovation in China. In H. Lee & L. Lim (Eds.), *Cultural policies in East Asia: Dynamics between state, arts and creative industries* (pp. 155–173). Palgrave Macmillan.

Kim, E., Fiore, A. M., & Payn, A. (2021). *Fashion trends: Analysis and forecasting* (2nd ed.). Bloomsbury Visual Arts.

Kim, A., MacInerney, P., Rüdiger Smith, T., & Yamakawa, N. (2020, June 29). *What makes Gen Z in Asia different?* McKinsey.com.

Lay, R. (2018). *Digital transformation—The ultimate challenge for the fashion industry*. Deloitte. www.deloitte.com.

Lefebvre, H., & Nicholson-Smith, D. (1991). *The production of space* (Vol. 142). Blackwell.

Li, C. (2021a). China's millennials: Navigating socioeconomic diversity and disparity in a digital era. In L. Chunling (Ed.), *China's youth: Increasing diversity amid persistent inequality* (pp. 1–38). Brookings Institution Press.

Li, C. (2021b). *China's youth: Persistent diversity amid persistent inequality*. Brookings Institution Press.

Lindgren, T. (2013). Chinese fashion designers in Shanghai: A new perspective. In S. Heaton (Ed.), *Fashioning identities: Cultures of exchange* (pp. 143–157). Inter-Disciplinary Press.

Ling, W., & Segre-Reinach, S. (2018). *Fashion in multiple Chinas: Chinese styles in the transglobal landscape*. I.B. Tauris.

Liu, F. (2011). *Urban youth in China: Modernity, the internet and the self*. Routledge.

Magana, G. (2018, July 6). Alibaba is piloting AI Fashion technology. *Business Insider*. https://www.businessinsider.com/alibaba-starts-using-fashion-ai-technology-2018-7?IR=T

McKinsey and Business of Fashion. (2020). *The State of fashion 2020*. https://www.businessoffashion.com/reports/news-analysis/the-state-of-fashion-2020-bof-mckinsey-report-releasedownload/

McKinsey. (2020a). *Understanding Chinese consumers: Growth engine of the world*. McKinsey.

McKinsey. (2020b, November 25). *China's Gen Z are coming of age: here is what marketers need to know*. McKinsey.

McKinsey. (2021). *The State of fashion 2021*. https://www.mckinsey.com/~/media/McKinsey/Industries/Retail/Our%20Insights/State%20of%20fashion/2021/The-State-of-Fashion-2021-vF.pdf

Nam, H., & Kannan, P. K. (2020). Digital environment in global markets: Cross-cultural implications for evolving customer journeys. *Journal of International Marketing, 28*(1), 28–47.

Oh, S., & Nah, K. (2022). Analysis of fashion value and emotion in digital environment based on analysis of famous Korean fashion YouTube review data. In T. Ahram & R. Taiar (Eds.), *Human interaction, emerging technologies and future systems* (pp. 240–245). Springer.

Pan, L. (2008). *Shanghai style: Art and design between the wars*. Long River Press.

Pan, L. (2009). Of Shanghai and Chinese cosmopolitanism. *Asian Ethnicity, 10*(3), 217–224.

People's Daily online. (2021, November 19). French brand L'Oréal under fire in China over delayed deliveries, misleading marketing.

Pompidou Center website. *Centre Pompidou x West Bund Museum Project Shanghai—Centre Pompidou*. https://www.centrepompidou.fr/

Potvin, J. (Ed.). (2009). *The places and spaces of fashion, 1800–2007*. Taylor & Francis.

Rocamora, A. (2009). *Fashioning the city: Paris, fashion and the media*. Bloomsbury.

Rogers, E. M. (2003). *Diffusion of innovations* (5th ed.). Free Press.

Soja, E. W. (2000). *Postmetropolis: Critical studies of cities and regions*. Wiley-Blackwell.

Throsby, D. (2008). The concentric circles model of the cultural industries. *Cultural Trends, 17*(3), 147–164.

Tsui, C. (2013a). *China fashion: Conversations with designers*. Bloomsbury.

Tsui, C. (2013b). From symbols to spirit: Changing conceptions of national identity in Chinese fashion. *Fashion Theory: The Journal of Dress, Body & Culture, 17*(5), 579–604.

Tsui. (2017, October 20). *What's the uniqueness of Post-90s designers? Christine Tsui*. www.christinetsui.org.

UNESCO. (2013). Creative Economy Report 2013 Special Edition.

United Nations. (2018). *World urbanization prospects: The 2018 revision*. https://population.un.org/wup/Publications/Files/WUP2018-KeyFacts.pdf

Van der Merwe, D. (2021). The metaverse as virtual heterotopia. *Conference Proceedings, 3rd World Conference on Social Sciences*, 22–24 October, Vienna.

Vogue Business in China. (2021, September 6). The four fashion personas of China's Gen Z. *Vogue.com*. https://www.voguebusiness.com/consumers/the-four-fashion-personas-of-chinas-gen-z

Wang, Z. (2022). Implementation of Chinese-styled branding in global fashion: 'Guochao' as a rising cultural identity. *Fashion, Style and Popular Culture, 9*(1–2), 149–183.

Wei, Z., Lee, M. Y., & Shen, H. (2018). What drives consumers in China to buy clothing online? Application of the technology acceptance model. *Journal of Textile and Fibrous Materials, 1*, 1–10.

Wu, Y. (2018). The rise of China with cultural soft power in the age of globalization. *Journal of Literature and Art Studies, 8*(5), 763–778.

CHAPTER 7

# Conclusion: The Collision of the Past and Future in China's Creative Industries: Local and Global Aspirations

*Sabine Chrétien-Ichikawa*

## 1 Foreword

Before the outbreak of the COVID-19 pandemic, I organized research seminars in a business school in Shanghai with the intention of creating a bridge between academics and the industry, and between Chinese and foreign experts. My own research and these scholarly experiences, which transcended the Chinese context while embracing the unique aspects of China, made me realize the importance of examining the country's burgeoning creative economy, as studied by Howkins (2001). Furthermore, I started attending an increasing number of conferences on digitalization, AI, and, more recently, the metaverse, all of which led me to realize that these advances are led by engineers who seem

S. Chrétien-Ichikawa (✉)
ESSCA School of Management, Shanghai, China
e-mail: sabine.ichikawa@essca.fr


S. Chrétien-Ichikawa and K. Pawlik (eds.), *Creative Industries and Digital Transformation in China*,
https://doi.org/10.1007/978-981-19-3049-2_7

to seldom consider the impact of their discoveries on society. At these conferences, when someone asked about presenters' potential responsibilities to society, some scientists replied: "*That is not my job*!" I was left with this reflection: Whose job is it then? Why shouldn't we all participate in this discussion? The idea for this book was partly inspired by these conversations and reflections.

This book is the fruit of long-lasting friendships and relations among people who share a deep interest in China, social transformation, culture and creativity. The first goal of this collaborative work was to gather the vision of European researchers in the social sciences who see China from within, as long-term residents, as opposed to observers who come for a few weeks of field research only, as is often the case. It is an attempt to bridge different worlds: the culture gap between the East and the West, academic and business mindsets, cultural and commercial goals in relation to art in particular, and individual and national interpretations of culture.

Upon reviewing our essays for this conclusion, I noticed that our independent explorations confirmed how much the growth of creative and cultural industries (CCIs) depends on specific conditions, embedded in China's unique historical and cultural context. It is not sufficient for China to follow the guidelines of international bodies, to launch new national cultural policies, to have a stable political context and institutional structures, to maintain a strong economic development, and to support a growing consumer demand. In fact, the development of intangible and cultural heritage, and in some cases, its rejuvenation, requires more time and immaterial skills than building tangible heritage such as cultural sites (UNESCO, 2003).

The Chinese environment faces challenges in using imported concepts and terms, such as CCIs, that do not match their reality. In spite of this dilemma, we chose Throsby's (2008) concentric model of cultural industries because it is a widely used model in international reports. Throsby's model posits that the individual creator or genius is central to the system, which does not take into account the collaborative nature of artistic or commercial creation, more common in collective societies (like China). For these reasons, we remain cautious about this terminology and categorization for the Chinese context. However, for the purposes of this book, the term CCIs serves to talk conjointly about interconnected sectors, such as television, film, music, publishing, video games, advertising, and fashion.

In our understanding, because CCIs rely on "human imagination" (Hesmondhalgh, 2018), they often bring together past and future dimensions of culture in deeper ways than other industries to find inspiration, meaning, and purpose. Artistic output, if allowed, can drive individual and collective paths, and influence the way a country is perceived, beyond national borders, acting as a form of soft power.

The Chinese context in which all the foreign-born authors of this book are immersed imposed challenges and constraints on our academic investigations, not found in our European countries of origin. Our essays did not have the ambition to be exhaustive, but rather we had the modest intention of uncovering some significant trends from our insiders' point of view in order to shed light on aspects of China that can have a global impact. In the future, we are eager to continue exploring the impact of Chinese CCIs on other industries, with a wider academic community, to follow and anticipate the influence of China's cultural expansion on the world.

## 2 Introduction

> To mobilize people, we need to understand and embrace their culture.—Ban Ki Moon (2013)

> Whether it be arts and crafts, books, films, paintings, festivals, songs, designs, digital animation or video games, the creative industries are more than just sectors with good economic growth performance and potential. They are expressions of the human imagination spreading important social and cultural values.—Mukhisa Kituyi (2018)

The economic competitiveness of a nation depends on its capacity to innovate and upgrade, as well as its economic and institutional structures, technology, sociocultural context, and history. China has the economic and financial means to surpass countries in several technological sectors, but the culturally defined dimensions that characterize CCIs cannot be imposed on people, nor managed with the same tools as other industries. Industries gain advantage through challenges, and benefit from rivals and demanding consumers (Porter, 1990). In a world of increasingly global competition, the image of nations become more important, and CCIs can foster soft power in unexpected and meaningful ways. As the need for creation and innovation increases, educational and institutional bodies, together with economic players, adapt and anticipate the demands of the knowledge economy. We are witnessing this context in the Chinese creative industries generally, and in Shanghai specifically. However, along with the tangible elements of CCIs, their success also stems from their ability to create values and dreams, to represent cultural identities, to influence and inspire, and to trigger social transformations. The arts covered in this book—among them art, calligraphy, music, dance, fashion, film, and games—are human expressions that emanate in different degrees from spiritual needs, emotional desires, talent, and creative explorations. They need space and time to blossom and their potential to change society is almost unlimited.

In 2013, the United Nations Creative Economy Report underlined several conditions for forging pathways for the arts in developing countries such as: the importance of rights for artists and creative entrepreneurs to protect their intellectual property; the contribution of creativity to inclusivity and sustainable societal development beyond CCIs' monetary value; the need for a culturally defined society; the connectedness between formal and informal sectors, systems, and networks (such as families in developing countries); and engaging in international exchange for mutual benefit. Our essays confirm several of these dimensions in the Chinese context and illustrate turning points, opportunities, challenges, and debates that are ongoing.

## 3 Key Arguments of the Chapters

Digitization is a thread that runs throughout all the chapters of this book. Ritter and Pedersen (2020) argued that digitization is not new, but the large quantities of data that are gathered nowadays require firms to develop new strategies. The authors define four phases of the development of digitization from 1990 to 2010, in which the post-2010 period, called "integration" and "digital as the new normal," is characterized by a widespread and accepted use of digital technologies. In the field of business-to-business issues, they defined digitalization as the application of digital technology to bring about the changes caused by digitization. In this book, we examined the influence of digitization in the field of Chinese CCIs at two levels: the national level and the urban context of major cities like Shanghai. We examined these two levels through exploring history, economy, politics, society, and culture, and we refer partly to the international framework of CCIs that does not necessarily fit the local culture, in order to highlight the unique context of China.

We reviewed some key factors of economic development since the country's 1980s economic reforms. For instance, the rise of the "Created in China" slogan as opposed to "Made in China" had profound repercussions on industrial decisions, and on CCIs specifically. Techno-culture and techno-nationalism have come to the forefront as drivers of economic and political power. The conversations between CCIs and the government translate into more restrictions such as reinforced censorship of culture and media, heightened moral concerns, and fears of filtered foreign influence. As explained in the chapters by Goretti and Chrétien-Ichikawa in particular, demographic factors are partially driving specific restrictions, especially the coming of age of hundreds of millions of millennials and Gen Z, and they impact the user's experiences of various art practices. Digital creative industries are an arm of China's competitive advantage globally, therefore gaming, among other CCIs, is increasingly monitored. This complex and moving environment gives rise to renewed debates, social concerns, and censorship, as Amadieu emphasized in his chapter on video games. The authors in this collection examine the ecology of art by establishing the link between culture, national identity, and soft power. Pawlik used calligraphy as a case study of one China's unique cultural practices and industries that are being shaped by digital technologies, with a potential impact on Chinese expressions of identity.

While many high-level governmental, institutional, and international forces are shaping the activities of China's CCIs, the authors of this volume also demonstrated how artists have exercised their agency in response to a dynamic arts scene. As explained by Ouairy, artists have navigated logistical issues such as acquiring studio space amid rising rents, moving from the center to the periphery of large cities like Shanghai. They also have had to figure out ways to address their complex local and national artistic movements and attempts at censorship in front of a growing international audience.

Since the 1980s, when foreign songs, TV dramas, movies, and popular cultural goods entered China, audiences discovered new ideas and lifestyles from several countries, from the West and from Japan. Some chapters focused on Shanghai city because of its status as the epitome of modernization in China and the site of an early pilot project for CCIs. Shanghai's history fuels symbolic capital in relation to all the creative industries housed there (O'Connor, & Gu 2014). Its specific international exposure and its role as the cradle of Chinese CCIs a hundred years ago have forged a different image from that of Beijing city, which represents a more official and traditional Chinese culture. In 2017, for instance, Beijing was ranked 4th in terms of competitiveness after Shanghai, Hong Kong, and Shenzhen, and 4th also in terms of cultural soft power (Jiansheng, 2019). Shanghai's nomination as a UNESCO Creative City, and its role as the host of the Shanghai World Expo less than 15 years ago, have accelerated the emergence of creative clusters in the city. However, the gentrification of many areas of Shanghai and the city's real estate boom have impacted the production and commercialization of art and artists' practices, including fashion.

Taken together, these chapters explore various facets of the arts scene in China and offer rich case studies of how artists, production studios, and large-scale industries like fashion and video games have navigated the competing interests presented by local, state, and international interests.

## 4 Challenges Ahead for Chinese CCIs, Domestically and Globally

The study of cultural industries usually starts from Theodor Adorno, who used this term along with Max Horkheimer in their 1947 essay "The Culture Industry: Enlightenment as Mass Deception" (Adorno & Horkheimer, 1979). Adorno wrote about film, radio, newspapers, jazz, and the popular music of his time. The message of his work was that art and culture had become absorbed by capitalist modes of production and the reception of art as a commodity. Furthermore, he underlined that technology enabled the reproducibility of art pieces that used to be unique, resulting in the industrialization of cultural goods. Scholarship reveals that currently Chinese art and business communities appear to be undergoing similar debates. Some see purpose in high culture and art forms, while others find an outlet in a rapidly evolving profit-driven mass culture offering a sea of opportunities. Could China demonstrate alternative paths to both options?

Politically, since CCIs influence people, as such they need to be compatible with national policies, whether cultural or economic. Zheng (2016) compared the link between art and culture in the 1920–1930s in Shanghai with the cultural policies of today, where the role of art in serving monetary interests raises questions for creative workers and intellectuals.

What lies ahead for creative industries can be foreseen partially by listening to the leaders' discourse. Since 2016, President Xi Jinping highlighted the need for cultural confidence. In 2021 he underlined that the nation needs to carry forward fine traditional culture, and that the success of socialism with Chinese characteristics is the result of a 5,000-year-old civilization (China Daily, 2021). In December 2021, "he expressed his hope that the writers and artists will bear in mind the national rejuvenation and the people, make innovations on the basis of tradition, better tell China's stories to the world, and stick to both moral integrity and artistic competence" (Xinhua, 2021). According to Xi, artists and writers should "grasp the contemporary theme of national rejuvenation and closely integrate the pursuit of their artistic life with the future of China, the destiny of the Chinese nation and the aspirations of the Chinese people" (Xinhua, 2021). The aspirations of the post-1990s creatives interviewed in the empirical research by Chrétien-Ichikawa did not reflect these official directions; nor did they mention promoting a national spirit, based on patriotism and reform. They did, however, express their objective to develop their own ideas and identity and to create unique Chinese brands. This confirms the opinion of Chinese fashion scholar Tsui (2017) who examined the rebellious spirit of young Chinese designers who studied abroad. Keane (2016) also argued that in China, creativity is weighted toward the aesthetic rather than toward disruptive forms, as is prevalent in the West. The Chinese government promotes a "harmonious society."

Appadurai (2004) argued that the culture of aspiration is related to affluence, and that seeing culture as the past and development as the future may create conflicts among poor populations. Furthermore, ideas of the future are embedded in culture. In the Chinese context, considering that poor populations are still prevalent in large provinces, and the relative "weakness" in soft power and cultural development (Nye, 2012),[1] the aspirations of some middle-class and affluent youth are changing society, and paving the way for the future of the country. The domestic market is fueled by an expanding middle-income group with a population of 400 million; it may take another 10–15 years to reach 800 million, reaching 60% of the population.

[1] President Hu Jintao in 2012 mentioned that Chinese culture was weak compared to Western culture. In Nye (2012).

Going global is the next challenge of Chinese CCIs. If we consider the moment in the future when CCIs could be exported abroad on a large scale, the conditions differ from the previous decades that made China an industrial and economic powerhouse. The export and development of CCIs require soft skills, individual and collective creative talent, innovative SMEs, and cultural content and values that can resonate with local and global audiences. After establishing large groups in the film, advertising, and games industries (such as Tencent, Alibaba, etc.) that all benefit from a strong local demand, the time of global expansion may create new challenges not yet addressed. To export Chinese CCIs' creative output, China may need to consider how other countries have succeeded in similar endeavors, either Europe and America, or Japan and South Korea, for instance. The cultural content of movies, music, and games from China is entering world markets, but it is still in an early phase. What are the conditions for its expansion?

Robust CCIs are at the forefront of proving China's status as a developed economy (Keane, 2016). The Chinese economic growth is still recent, and its cultural impact in the world is not yet a major research topic, but it is only a question of years. The underlying reason may be that its culture, prior to the expansion of CCIs, has not yet matched the power of its economy, industry, and manufacturing sectors. However, the rapid technological transformation and digital revolution are changing the potential of China to conquer other markets. CCIs specifically require cultural content that echo people's desires, aspirations, and dreams. Can China respond to global consumer needs? The country's transition to outputting intangible products and culturally defined content is posing new challenges that have still not been fully addressed. The investment in cultural creation requires an adaptation both from the producer side and from the user side. In China, the policies and laws that regulate production and consumption may need to be revisited.

In conclusion, China is striving on the economic, political, technological, and cultural fronts, with a growing impact on world affairs and global markets. The complexity of understanding the dynamics shaping this civilization, culture, and nation is an overwhelming task. We humbly hope this book will contribute to more exchanges between international communities in academia and education, as well as among creative and cultural industries, in order to anticipate and forge "our common future" (WCED, 1987).

## References


Adorno, T., & Horkheimer, M. (1979). Dialectic of Enlightenment, trans. *J. Cumming*. Verso.

Appadurai, A. (2004). The capacity to aspire: Culture and the terms of recognition. In V. Rao & M. Walton (Eds.), *Culture and public action* (pp. 59–84). Stanford University Press.

China Daily. (2021, March 24). President emphasizes cultural confidence. *China Daily*. anhuinews.com

Hesmondhalgh, D. (2018). *The cultural industries* (4th ed.). Sage.

Howkins, J. (2001). *Creative economy: How people make money from ideas*. Penguin Books.

Jiansheng, L. (2019). Building a national cultural center in the context of the new Beijing urban master plan. In Beijing Academy of Social Sciences (Eds.), *Analysis of the development of Beijing in 2018* (pp. 143–185). Palgrave Macmillan.

Keane, M. (Ed.). (2016). *Handbook of cultural and creative industries in China*. Edward Elgar Publishing.

Nye, Joseph S. (2012, January 17). Why China is weak on soft power. *New York Times*.

O'Connor, J., & Gu, X. (2014). Creative industry clusters in Shanghai: A success story? *International journal of cultural policy*, *20*(1), 1–20.

Porter, M. E. (1990, March–April). The competitive advantage of nations. *Harvard Business Review*.

Ritter, T., & Pedersen, C. L. (2020). Digitization capability and the digitalization of business models in business-to-business firms: Past, present, and future. *Industrial Marketing Management*, *86*, 180–190.

Throsby, D. (2008). The concentric circles model of the cultural industries. *Cultural Trends*, *17*(3), 147–164.

Tsui, C. (2017, October 20). *What's the uniqueness of post-90s designers? Christine Tsui*. www.christinetsui.org.

UNESCO. (2003). 2003 Convention for the safeguarding of Intangible Cultural Heritage. *Sixth session of the intergovernmental committee for the safeguarding of the intangible cultural heritage* (pp. 22–29). https://ich.unesco.org/doc/src/18440-EN.pdf. Accessed November 2011.

United Nations Creative Economy Report. (2013). United Nations Creative Economy Report, 2013. http://www.creativeeconomyreport2013.com/

WCED World Commission on Environment and Development. (1987). *Brundtland Report*.

Xinhua. (2021, December 15). Xi stresses cultural confidence at major conference of artists, writers—China.org.cn.

Zheng, J. (2016). Chapter 35: A comparative perspective on the industrialization of art in the Republican period in Shanghai and today's creative industry clusters. In M. Keane (Ed.), *Handbook of cultural and creative industries in China* (pp. 519–532). Edward Elgar Publishing.

# Index




S. Chrétien-Ichikawa and K. Pawlik (eds.), *Creative Industries and Digital Transformation in China*,
https://doi.org/10.1007/978-981-19-3049-2

The manufacturer's authorised representative in the EU is Springer Nature Customer Service Centre GmbH, Europaplatz 3, 69115 Heidelberg, Germany. If you have any concerns regarding our products, please contact ProductSafety@springernature.com

Printed and bound by CPI Group (UK) Ltd, Croydon, CR0 4YY

30/09/2026

02225260-0015